AUROVILLE ARCHITECTURE

towards new forms for a new consciousness

Acknowledgements

John Mandeen, Other photos have been contributed by individual architects;
Auroville Archives (Auroville's early years); Dominique Darr;
Giorgio (the Matrimandir interior and Inner Chamber).

Copyright : Prisma, Auroville
Author : Franz Fassbender
Photographs : John Mandeen

Fifth edition

ISBN 978-93-95460-49-1 (Paperpack)
ISBN 978-93-95460-90-3 (ebook)

BISAC Code:
ARC024000, ARCHITECTURE / Buildings / General
ARC005000, ARCHITECTURE / History / General
ARC007000, ARCHITECTURE / Interior Design / General
ARC015000, ARCHITECTURE / Professional Practice
ARC012000, ARCHITECTURE / Reference
ARC020000, ARCHITECTURE / Regional
ARC013000, ARCHITECTURE / Study & Teaching
ARC025000, ARCHITECTURE / Vernacular

Thema Subject Category:
AM, Architecture
AMA, Theory of architecture
AMC, Architectural structure and design
AMR, Architecture: interior design
AMX, History of architecture
AMV, Landscape architecture and design
AMCR, Environmentally-friendly ('green') architecture and design
AMD, Architecture: professional practice

Cataloging-in-Publication Data for this title is available from the Library of Congress.

Published by:
PRISMA, an imprint of Digital Media Initiatives
PRISMA, Aurelec / Prayogshala,
Auroville 605101, Tamil Nadu, India
www.prisma.haus

INDIA
Auroville

Foreword

This book presents an explanatory introduction to the variety of architectural approaches taken since Auroville's founding in 1968, while at the same time giving an opportunity to many of the township's practicing architects to talk about their work, their inspiration and future vision.

Although we hope the brochure acts as a source of inspiration to all those interested in architecture, both within India and abroad, it does not set out to present any detailed analysis of Auroville architecture.

Photos on left:

Photos from Auroville's early days

Auroville's symbol

The Auroville symbol was given by the Mother on 16.7.71. In approving the drawing she gave the following explanation:

"The dot at the centre represents Unity, the Supreme; the inner circle represents the creation, the conception of the City; the petals represent the power of expression, realisation."

Contents

A Dream 6
Auroville and its architectural journey 8
Auroville concept and
inauguration 10
A model future township 13
Architecture and urban development 14
Meet the architect..................................18
Early town planning 24
Early Aspiration settlement 32
Early creative and experimental
architecture 38
The Soul of the City...............................46
Amphitheatre 50
Research in architecture 52
Planning the township 54
The location
of the four zones 55
Decoding the Galaxy..............................56

International Zone 58
Bharat Nivas, Pavilion of India 60
Sri Aurobindo Auditorium 63
Kala Kendra 64
SAWCHU...65
Centre for Indian Culture.......................66
Atithi Griha Guest House 68
International House.................................70
Pavilion of Tibetan Culture 72
The Unity Pavilion..................................73
Hall of Peace 75
Savitri Bhavan 76
Savitri Bhavan Hostel 80

Industrial Zone 82
Upasana 82
Auromode...83
CSR 83

Cultural Zone 84
Kalabhumi 84
CRIPA - Centre for Research in the
Performing Arts 85

Residential Zone 86
Samasti...86
Prarthna and Sukhavati Invocation 87
Samasti and Grace settlement...............88
Grace 89
Vikas 90

Surrender 90
Creativity...91
Citadines 92
Luminosity 94
Swayam...96
Realization 100
Arati III 102
Maitreye 103
Maitreye II 104
Inspiration...105
Prayathna II 106

Public buildings 108
Visitors Centre 108
Town Hall..112
Multimedia Centre................................115
Mitra Youth Hostel 116
SAIIER 117
Arka 119
Institute for Integral Health 120
The Auroville Library 121
Solar Kitchen 122
Pour Tous Distribution Centre 124

SAIIER schools 126
Kindergarten 126
Progress Landscape 126
After School 126
Transition School..................................128
Future School 129
New Era Secondary School..................130
Super School building 131
The Pyramids 131
Deepanam School 131
Last School 132
Aikiyam School 134
Udavi School 134
La Piscine 135
Ilaignarkal Education Centre................135
Nandanam Kindergarten and Crèche 135
Arka 136
Kuyilapalayam School...........................136
Bommaiyapalayam School 136
Pitanga Hall 137
Auroville Health Centre 138
Quiet Healing Centre 139

Other buildings 141
Aurelec – Prayogashala 141

Aureka 141
Lines of Force.......................................142
Water Tower..142
Vérité Integral Learning Centre 143
Vérité Yoga Hall 144
Road Service...145

Guest houses 146
Afsanah Guest House 146
Centre Guest House 147
Samasti Guest House 148
Atithi Griha 148
Gaia's Garden Guest House..................148
Fraternity Guest House 148

Profiles of architects 150
Roger Anger 150
Piero & Gloria Cicionesi 155
André Hababou......................................159
Poppo Pingel...162
Peter Anderschitz 166
Ajit & Ratna Koujalgi.............................167
Helmut Schmid......................................168
Suhasini Ayer-Guigan 170
Rolf Redis 172
Mona Doctor-Pingel 174
Satprem Maïni 180
Sigi Keller 182
Gundolf Zurmühl 183
Sonali Phadnis 184
Shama Dalvi 187
Dharmesh Jadeja..................................188
Pino Marchese 192
Sheril Castelino 193
David Nightingale & Ganesh Bala 194
Ray Meeker 196
Shailaja Sudhalkar Bhati 198
Ananda..200
Meera Prajapati 201
Anita 202
Poonam Mulchandani 203
SacredGroves 204
Fabian Ostner.......................................206

Architects who have
contributed to Auroville 208
Anupama Kundoo 208
Dominic Dube 210
Jana Dreikhausen 212

A Dream

There should be somewhere upon earth a place that no nation could claim as its sole property, a place where all human beings of goodwill, sincere in their aspiration, could live freely as citizens of the world, obeying one single authority, that of the supreme Truth; a place of peace, concord, harmony, where all the fighting instincts of man would be used exclusively to conquer the causes of his suffering and misery, to surmount his weakness and ignorance, to triumph over his limitations and incapacities; a place where the needs of the spirit and the care for progress would get precedence over the satisfaction of desires and passions, the seeking for pleasures and material enjoyments.

In this place, children would be able to grow and develop integrally without losing contact with their soul. Education would be given, not with a view to passing examinations and getting certificates and posts, but for enriching the existing faculties and bringing forth new ones. In this place titles and positions would be supplanted by opportunities to serve and organize. The needs of the body will be provided for equally in the case of each and everyone. In the general organisation intellectual, moral and spiritual superiority will find expression not in the enhancement of the pleasures and powers of life but in the increase of duties and responsibilities.

Artistic beauty in all forms, painting, sculpture, music, literature, will be available equally to all, the opportunity to share in the joys they bring being limited solely by each one's capacities and not by social or financial position.

For in this ideal place money would be no more the sovereign lord. Individual merit will have a greater importance than the value due to material wealth and social position. Work would not be there as the means of gaining one's livelihood, it would be the means whereby to express oneself, develop one's capacities and possibilities, while doing at the same time service to the whole group, which on its side would provide for each one's subsistence and for the field of his work.

In brief, it would be a place where the relations among human beings, usually based almost exclusively upon competition and strife, would be replaced by relations of emulation for doing better, for collaboration, relations of real brotherhood.

– The Mother

Auroville and its architectural journey

At the beginning, in a small town called Pondicherry (now Puducherry) with its chequered history of colonial rulers from the Dutch, Portuguese, English and finally the French, there lived a lady who dreamed an impossible dream, a dream of an international city dedicated to human unity. She envisaged the city as a laboratory, a laboratory wherein to work on a change of consciousness, where the urban planning and architecture would embody this fusion of matter and spirit, past and future, a cradle for the new human society. She chose an architect to visualise her ideal city who, after working through several ideas and concepts, inspired by a 4 petal flower-like plan drawn by her in June 1965, zeroed in on a concept that has since been called the "galaxy concept". The architect was Roger Anger, and the creatrix of this audacious project was the Mother.

Roger Anger, emerging from the late 1940s movement of the "Academy of Architecture" from Ecole des Beaux-Arts, where the emphasis was on art and sculpture, on the interpenetration of forms, on "speaking architecture" with symbolism and shapes, with his designs for houses and schools in the Auromodele community area in the early 1970s set the tone for Auroville architecture for the next 2 decades. These works of non-rectilinear form, coupled with his position, built up a perception that truly creative architecture could never be "rectilinear". A habitat seeking to be a "home for the consciousness of the future" could only be manifested in shapes that were divorced from the geography, culture and sociology of the place. In short a house cannot be house-like in appearance if it has to capture the essence of the new human society.

In parallel, due to the imperative need to create shelter for the people and projects that were sprouting across the landscape, the first two decades of Auroville were also a period of incredible innovation by non-architects, self-building using local building technologies and materials flavoured by influences of the time (1960s and '70s) and the cultural diversity of the first inhabitants. Using casuarinas as frames, covered with plaited coconut fronds called locally "keet", incredible living forms and spaces were created. Large hives of multi-user space built during this period housed the first Aurovilians in this desiccated and barren landscape. These inclusive and open decades, coupled with an exuberant social setting, unleashed extreme creativity, not seen since.

By the end of the 1980s, architects like Piero and Gloria had executed a series of houses in Certitude settlement designed with built forms in the international style, while Poppo was experimenting with materials and forms inspired from the vernacular, and the architects and designers who had worked in Roger Anger's studio "Auroville's Future", having imbibed his passion for expressionist form, were trying their hand at re-interpreting the built form, using the new wonder material called "ferrocement" to fool the physics of gravity, thermodynamics and surface tension. But unfortunately for both, the vegetal and ferrocement have proved unable to survive the tyranny of the tropics.

Meanwhile the name "Auroville", by the early 1990s, had become synonymous with "architecture" due to targeted exposure in print media in a country that was emerging from a socialist era to a globalised economy. With the construction boom in the country, the demand for architects soared and the number of schools of architecture exploded from a handful to hundreds all over the country. There were over 60+ schools of Architecture in the state of Tamil Nadu alone as at March 2013, and all these institutions started to look towards Auroville as the preferred destination for their field trips, drawn by the reputation built up by the "green and sustainable design" works of the Auroville architects in the 1980-90s, integrating renewable energy, water management, earth construction and appropriate building materials and technology with built forms well anchored in the geography and climate of the place. Yet once these groups reached their destination, they were drawn towards the non-rectilinear and temperate climate forms, confirming that the attraction to the exotic is inbuilt into the human psyche even at the cost of long term sustainability.

In the new millennium, with the completion of the Matrimandir, as the development of the city becomes imperative, Auroville's resident architects face the twin challenge of producing built forms that should be embedded within an undefined future urban context, simultaneously self-conscious of the greatness imposed on them as they produce anxious non-denominational forms. Some of the recent public housing projects best express this anxiety to distance themselves from the past, while the future remains elusive due to the diversity of expression inherent in a multicultural society. And yet, the quality of built expression and its integration within its environment, as it is presently in Auroville, is still inspirational compared to the rest of the country.

Suhasini Ayer-Guigan

Auroville's concept and inauguration

Auroville is a universal township in the making for a population of up to 50,000 people from around the world.

The purpose of Auroville is to realise human unity without sacrificing diversity. Today Auroville is recognised as the first and only internationally endorsed ongoing experiment in human unity and transformation of consciousness, also concerned with – and practically researching into – sustainable living and the future cultural, environmental, social and spiritual needs of mankind. Auroville was founded on 28th February 1968 when some 5,000 people assembled near the banyan tree at the centre of the future township for an inauguration ceremony attended by representatives of 124 nations, including all the States of India. The representatives brought with them some soil from their home land, to be mixed in a white marble-clad, lotus-shaped urn, now sited at the focal point of the Amphitheatre. At the same time Auroville was given its 4-point Charter by its founder, French-born Mira Alfassa, known as the Mother, who was the spiritual collaborator of India's great philosopher-yogi Sri Aurobindo.

The Auroville Charter reads as follows:

1. Auroville belongs to nobody in particular. Auroville belongs to humanity as a whole. But to live in Auroville one must be a willing servitor of the Divine Consciousness.
2. Auroville will be the place of an unending education, of constant progress, and a youth that never ages.
3. Auroville wants to be the bridge between the past and the future. Taking advantage of all discoveries from without and from within, Auroville will boldly spring towards future realisations.
4. Auroville will be a site of material and spiritual researches for a living embodiment of an actual Human Unity.

At the same time the Mother issued the following invitation to the world at large to come and manifest the township in an appropriate spirit:

Greetings from Auroville to all men of goodwill. Are invited to Auroville all those who thirst for progress and aspire to a higher and truer life.

The project is guided by this ideal. The overall concept of the town provides for a material focus, the Matrimandir, surrounded by four zones - the Cultural, International, Industrial and Residential, all contained within a large surrounding Green Belt.

At the centre is the Matrimandir, a place for silent concentration and the development of a union with the divine manifesting in a progressive human unity.

In the **International Zone**, the national pavilions will present in a living manner the deep unity of nations and people while at the same time celebrating their cultural diversity. It is also planned to build there a research institute, the Centre for International Research in Human Unity (CIRHU), with the aim of it becoming a forum for conceiving and initiating plans of action designed to develop human unity.

In the **Industrial Zone**, the place for manufacture of goods and generation of money for this intended self-supporting city, the emphasis will not be on competitive productivity alone.

In the **Residential Zone**, there will be low as well as relatively high-density accommodation with environmentally appropriate designs supportive of easy communication between the residents.

In the **Cultural Zone** will be located the main infrastructure for an education which will not be given with a view to passing examinations, but rather to support the growth of the soul and facilitate the discovery of the inner unity between human beings.

This zone will also house artistic and cultural facilities, including a theatre, and a comprehensive sports complex with running track, etc.

The Mother

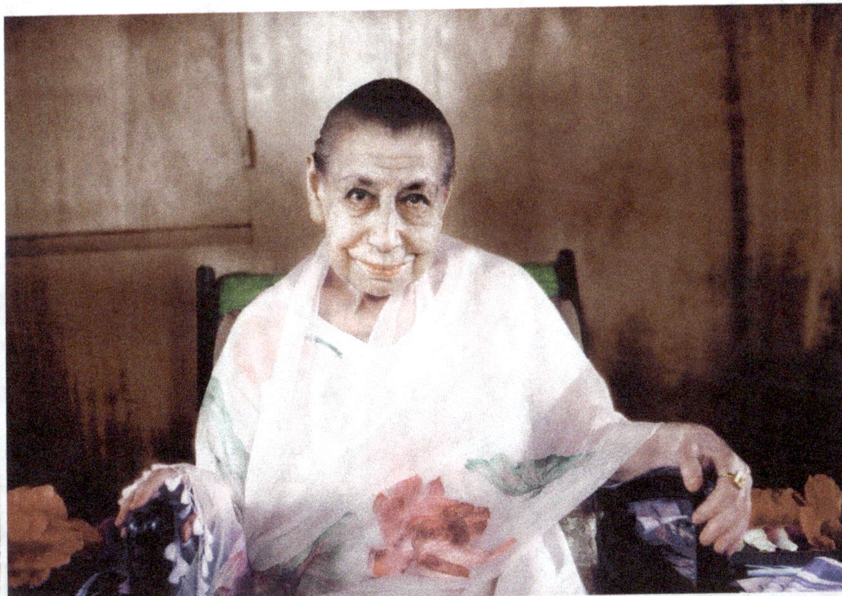

Auroville inauguration ceremony 28.2.68

A model future township

In terms of physical development, Auroville aims at becoming a model of the 'city of the future', or 'the city the earth needs'. It wants to show the world that future realisations in all fields of work will allow us to build beautiful cities where people sincerely looking towards a more harmonious future will want to live.

But, what should be the "City of the Future"?

Auroville's founder, the Mother, gave clear parameters for a number of things, while for other things she gave a free hand to the Chief Architect, Roger Anger of France, who had been appointed by her to oversee the township's physical development.

Some 30+ years after her demise, and after a lot of changes in Auroville, India and the world, where are we today?

In some respects, we think we know what this 'city of the future' should be; in other respects we only know what it shouldn't be; and again, in other respects, we simply don't know at all. We know that, on a conceptual level, the city has already been 'seen' and is simply waiting to manifest. Our work is to be receptive enough to make that happen.

Architect's dream
The architecture expressed by the dreams and aspirations of a nation or a community stands as an expression of its core values in matter, and the multiplicity of styles and typologies found in Auroville reflect the socio-economic, cultural, ideological, ecological and climatic factors that have shaped us over three decades. They present a visual history of our development and evolution for all to see.

Pioneering stage
The buildings of the first decade, which was Auroville's pioneering stage, adopted the vernacular building materials of casuarina, keet, palm leaf and thatch. The builders took these construction materials to high forms of self-expression and imagination, and worked in close collaboration with the local artisans. The large 'Aspiration' settlement is a lively testament to the durability of the structures created at that time. At the same time, alongside these buildings ultra-modern shaped buildings like Last School, After School and today's Pyramids Art Centre were also coming up in stark contrast.

Creative revolution
At the same time, the push to experiment for 'community living' as a step towards the future city gave rise to 'Auromodèle', a communal living area which still remains an architectural exposition of forms and shapes that break the mould of the conventional principle of 'four walls and a roof' habitation. These beginnings provoked a creative revolution in the self-builders of the 70's and early 80's in experimenting with building materials, technology, design and life-styles.

Applied research
One of the results of this period was serious applied research, and the last decade and a half has seen considerable advances in ferrocement technology for roofs and interior fittings as well as compressed earth blocks for load bearing structures. Some of the buildings constructed using these materials have won national design awards and significant grants-in-aid from agencies that support such innovations.

Original 'Galaxy' Town Plan

Architecture and urban development

The project of Auroville was conceived by the Mother as an urban experiment to undertake the work of "evolution of consciousness" in a society that would concretely experiment with the challenges of economy, sociology, environment and culture within an urban context while seeking a spiritual life. When she talked about her ideal city she was encompassing the complexity of an urban society into the experiment, unlike many of the idealistic communes, settlements and ashrams that live a life of order, serenity and peace with a limited range of activities and social groupings.

In 1964, the Mother sketched the shape of her city with four zones or sections - the Industrial, Cultural, Residential and International - indicating the urban context of the project. She chose the French architect Roger Anger to be the chief architect of this project. He presented several schemes and interpretations of the Mother's concept in the period 1965-67, from which the "Galaxy" plan emerged and was accepted by the Mother. In this concept, following the Mother's original sketch, the city has been divided into four zones around the Matrimandir and its gardens. A green belt all around the city would provide it with protection and the sustenance required by its residents. The circulation inside the city was envisaged to be via a system of ring and radial roads.

However, the conceptual planning was done without any reference to the site conditions, as the exact location had yet to be identified. The initial location considered was quite near Usteri Lake, both sides of the Tindivanam-Pondicherry highway. However, Roger Anger persuaded the Mother to drop this site because of the problems likely to arise from having a major highway cutting through the middle of the city. The next choice was Auroville's present location. Therefore, the Galaxy plan had not taken into account the geo-physical conditions of topography, climate, existing traditional settlements and villages within the designated township area.

After formal launching of the project on 28th February 1968, the reality of the area had to be incorporated. Roger Anger, realising the complexity of the project, started to create two first settlements: Auromodèle and Aspiration. Auromodèle was intended as a model for the township to be. Aspiration was necessary to house the first settlers in simple accommodation. The Matrimandir was started in 1971, and Bharat Nivas, the Pavilion of India, shortly after.

In 1973, the Mother passed away, and Auroville then went through a protracted period of difficulties with the original nurturing body, the Sri Aurobindo Society in Pondicherry. This culminated in intervention by the Government of India in 1980. In consequence of these difficulties, there was slow population growth and only a few random housing settlements emerged within the township area. Progress in construction of the Matrimandir was also slow, and at Bharat Nivas work stopped completely.

In 1988, the Government of India passed the Auroville Foundation Act, giving a unique status and protection to the project. One feature of this Act was that it required a Master Plan to be made. This was done, and the Master Plan for "The Auroville Universal Township" was approved by the Ministry of Human Resource Development, Government of India, on 12th April 2001. On the basis of this document the community of Auroville was expected to produce a 5-year development plan with projects for approval and funding.

The responsibility for planning and development of the township today is with L'Avenir d'Auroville. The name "L'Avenir d'Auroville" or "Auroville's Future" was given by the Mother to the original planning and development office of Roger Anger. L'Avenir d'Auroville has presently 12 members who look after the work areas of planning (6), development (2), administration (2) and communication (2).

L'Avenir' d'Auroville, whose responsibilities include the preparation of detailed urban plans on the basis of the approved Master Plan, is a working group constituted by Auroville's Residents Assembly. It is a body representative of the various interested groups that have emerged: the Zonal Groups that coordinate, scrutinise, monitor and promote development in the industrial, cultural, residential and international zones; the Green Group, a working group dealing with the Green Belt and forest and farm development; the Matrimandir group; and units working with water, energy and sanitation management, or which are involved in regional outreach programmes with the local villages.

The main challenge for any group involved with planning and development of Auroville is to accommodate the developmental needs of the present population with the means available today, while plugging in to the grand dream that is represented by the "galaxy concept". All developmental projects are being realised with donations and grants in aid from the Aurovilians, governmental and non-governmental funding agencies, Auroville International centres around the world, and various individual philanthropists. Therefore the type of project envisaged, its scale, and how it relates to the overall matrix of development is often an enigma, even to the people who are supposed to initiate and manage the planning of Auroville.

Today, the architectural richness and diversity that is evident to most visitors to Auroville impresses them, but at the same time they are left puzzled by the lack of the "township" that the publications of Auroville extol. The impression that most visitors get is of isolated developments connected by dirt roads in a forest of trees. Housing, the service sector, and infrastructure like roads, energy and water resources, are either insufficient or poorly funded thanks to this skewed motor of development. There are public projects that are designed and built for a future population of 50,000 persons, while the present population of only around 2,200 people is expected to use and pay for their operation and maintenance costs, creating an economic burden on the community. At the same time, schools, health services, banking, housing, work spaces and jobs are stretched to their limits to meet the needs of the present population. The 2–5% growth rate of population over the last 25 years, insufficient economic growth, non-availability of land and the scattered nature of settlement development, add to the complexity of planning for Auroville.

The socio-economic diversity of the population, while providing a richly varied society, also throws up problems of communication and decision-making in any participatory planning exercise. Due to historical reasons the development of Auroville has happened in a dispersed and fragmented fashion since its inception. Today, to integrate and intensify these developments within the Master Plan is not easy, as it leads to conflicts of land use and density between the planners, existing settlements / residents and proposed projects. Also, the planners and administrators have to grapple with the issues of water and watershed management for a township to develop, as the area is becoming more water-scarce through increased demand from the entire region, fuelled by the suburban and industrial growth of Pondicherry, the farming subsidy for energy and water, and the population growth in villages around Auroville. The environmental awareness within Auroville is exemplary, compared to most similar population groups, but issues such as equitable development, co-management and sharing of essential resources are not easy to deal with on a human level. The architects, planners and urban management professionals of Auroville have, over the last 20+ years, been actively working on projects within the community requiring energy-efficient and green buildings, water and sanitation management using decentralised and low input systems, and renewable energy systems. There are several prototype projects that are demonstrating the use of alternative building materials and technology, innovative design solutions, and even settlements that integrate most of these components.

The next challenge that Auroville has to tackle on its path to becoming a full township is how to transfer all this experimentation and innovation onto an urban scale to create sustainable urban development that can answer the global challenge of this century - "environmentally and socio-economically sustainable cities and towns." We are moving towards a world where more than half the population lives in urban areas, and the impact of the brown issues are more than the green issues, with the growing competition for natural resources between the countryside and the city. Is Auroville going to emulate the conventional urban format, where the ecological footprint is going to be 3-4 times the township area, or are we going to be truly the cradle of the superman, who will live a life rich in diversity in harmony with the environment? These are not easy questions to answer or tasks to undertake, but this is part of the challenge of the "new consciousness" Auroville aspires to manifest.

LIFE

Meet the Architect

Early interview with Roger Anger, the architect of Auroville, 1968

Q: Auroville may be said to be the progressive manifestation of the vision of a great psychologist and sociologist, Sri Aurobindo. That manifestation is thrust forward by the Mother's realising power and shaped by the technique and arts of our time. As you, Roger Anger, are the originator of Auroville's architectural conception, we would first like to know you better: what was your activity up to now? ...what creative principles do you follow?

R.A.: Very kind of you to ask, but such questions are relatively unimportant: what I will be as Auroville's architect will certainly differ to a great extent from what I have been up to now. If, at present, the responsibility of Auroville rests on me, my strong intention is to open the doors widely to other architects. In France, a group has already been formed and is at work on the project. The universal nature of Auroville calls for the meeting of different trends of architectural creation in order that the city may become a true planetary achievement. Well, if I must... about myself... like any French architect I studied at the "Beaux Arts". Very soon I had the opportunity to build a good number of spectacular projects. In France I am considered as belonging, not to a revolutionary, but to an "avant garde" architectural trend. At the beginning of my career, I was very much concerned with the renewal of shape, with an architecture very strongly centred around the study of space. For a certain number of years now I have been led to devote myself to an architecture concerned with man viewed as a social being and to conceive a kind of' architecture with which man would actually be merged. The group of architects I am working with is studying pan-social architectural forms. They constitute a preview of the flexible type of architecture necessary for Auroville's first modules and could meet the dynamic imperatives of its construction through the years. Inevitably, I became more and more interested in the principles of urbanism and have utilized them for Auroville's successive layouts and, even more so, in the latest model of the town.

Q: Would you agree with Equals One's (=I) opinion that the first object of a town is to facilitate the meeting of man with man?

R.A.: Obviously yes. Just as obviously, it has been forgotten in the recent past. It is inconceivable that we could forget it. In order to achieve the integration of man within his social community, we had to rediscover what made those small towns of southern Europe successful—they were so beautiful and the inhabitants were happy living in them. One reason for their success came from their construction on slopes: one could discover constantly new viewpoints, new angles for seeing space and shapes. Another reason is that they not only offered a dynamically permanent environment but also an environment adapted to man's dimensions. In our effort to bring together all these factors of success we developed a concept of urbanism now called "volumetric". "Volumetric urbanism" consists in recreating on selected artificial sites progressive levels with multiple perspectives. The town consists of a macrostructure, created with terraces on successive levels, that looks like a real pyramid when stripped to its essentials. The pyramid is fitted on its exterior planes with levels of habitation which give an extraordinary contact with nature. Inside, one finds a complete complex of things necessary for living: cultural and recreation centres, commercial outlets, etc. The pyramid's vertical axis contains systems of high speed elevators and escalators offering quick circulation with and between the levels and easy communication to residential sectors. Such a pyramid constitutes a complete organic unit for ten to fifteen thousand inhabitants. When several are positioned on the ground, interconnected by causeways, a growth pattern is established which could finally contain half a million people. Each unit enjoys naturally its own life and relations with others. The number of people in each organic unit is limited so that intimate human relations remain possible, so that a kind of open fraternity may exist, a necessity in the town of the future. We feel that an important number of contacts between individuals is so necessary for a balanced community existence that, with the help of modern technology, we conceived an architecture which aims at inducing this cohesion, this warm mutuality. In short, we start with artificial platforms, terraces on which we have positioned a highly concentrated habitat.

Running against this conception, modern western urbanism for the last twenty five years has been geometric, horizontal—it has killed human relations and been a dramatic failure. People are isolated, lost, within a living unit neither self-sufficient nor self-contained, separated from others by lawns and linear lots. Redensification is today's necessity. Citizens of these new cities may enjoy once again (as was the case with streets and forums of the past), the dialogue of man with man.

Q: What field does Auroville offer for your urban research?

R.A.: Auroville is positioned on the Coromandel coast at a place where land is relatively flat. We intend to build artificial levels, a circular macrostructure which will give the town its outlook and will constitute the highest densification zone. Approximately twenty five thousand people will live in this "ring". It will not be an opaque mass but will offer, on the contrary, many transactions, fantastic views from outside to inside and vice-versa. We will create shade-architecture (a must in a tropical climate), that will allow for undercover traffic and sudden outbursts of light within patios and elevated gardens. Within this ring a bustling life will exist, the town's vital soul.

The ring—itself encircled by a hundred-metre-wide canal where artificial islands will provide a rhythm, a dwelling place for various aquatic birds, where 21st century gondolas will leisurely circumnavigate—will be the intersection of all sectors, the town's centripetal focus. This is where, in addition to the fairy-like charm of canals, the main commercial centre will be located. Here one will find theatres, sports-grounds, recreation halls, gardens for meditation, forums for meetings, hotels... Visitors galore, of course, since Auroville is not a closed town, but a town open to the world and the urbanist must never forget this essential openness.

Q: What have you planned to facilitate the meeting of man with man?

R.A.: Auroville will attempt the rehabilitation of streets, a change from rush-ways to a satisfying and happy system of circulation for man, from meeting place to meeting place: squares, fountains, gardens, pools, staircases, wings of shade, sudden shafts of sunlight, perspectives, auditoriums, amphitheatres, theatres, sports-grounds, research and leisure centres, restaurants and shops.

In the residential zone these streets, with all their meeting places, will become arteries for creative neighbourhoods (not dormitories) of people enjoying some particular common activity that will be their distinctive mark, a source for unique offerings to others. In the central ring, other meeting places will be found to accommodate several such groups. Finally, in the cultural zone, installations will be built where the whole town may enjoy festivities with as many as a hundred thousand present.

Q: Auroville is being deliberately conceived as an experimental town. What does that imply from the urbanist's viewpoint?

R.A.: Auroville will be a totally unprecedented psychological, social, educational and architectural experiment which, as with all experiments, might reveal errors. In truth not errors, but lacunae in man's urban consciousness. We would like Auroville to be a progressive, an evolving town, full of meaning, never to be "finished."

This continual growth does not refer to the number of inhabitants, which will not exceed fifty thousand, but to an evolution of the physical body, of the life of Auroville, of its society and also of its genius. This is why the most plastic formula will be the best from the urbanist's viewpoint. Here, by the way, we come to

Nebula model study sketch including roofs with solar panels, 1966 what will be the principle of tomorrow's urbanism: giving the town basic lines of power, main penetration channels, through a macrostructure that shapes the outlook and facilitates an inner direction. Then, just as with a bottle-rack, a mobile microstructure is fitted in, and can he changed, modified according to the needs of the town, the zone, as well as the individuals. Urbanism cannot be separated from plastic, open-ended architectural vision, Both are striving after an environment where man can live and evolve with joy. A macrostructure, like a mountain, cannot easily be changed. The macrostructure is an arrangement of space involving an underworld of sewage pipes, of water and electricity connections, main circulation ways wandering through the surface relief, natural or artificial climatic conditions bathing the whole complex. Once the macrostructure is positioned, everything becomes possible. In this structure is laid an outer skin, changeable and plastic so that it may be stretched, so that its colour may suddenly be altered all along an avenue by a play, let us say, of revolving panels. Such an approach is the only one that will allow an evolution of the town in time and within a given space. The clothing of' the town may be changed, renewed without drastic destruction.

Q: Has Auroville already evolved, even before starting to take a physical body?

R.A.: Naturally! Several successive layouts have already been made and each represents a different stage of a consistent conception. In fact, we would like to allow Auroville to materialize according to its own dynamism so that a real communion establishes itself between those who will live in Auroville and those who will create it. This is for architects one of the most difficult problems to solve. Anyhow, we have no intention of building arbitrarily. Not even one single area will conform to an exclusive architectural design. Many different teams must be at work and collaborate, each contributing very different expressions, under the coordination of a group empowered to unify this diversity.

Q: Auroville's construction will start in 1968. What other urbanistic problems can you mention?

R.A.: Auroville's main lines of strength have been determined for a long time: the main penetration ways, the ring and the four great sectors (residential, cultural, industrial and international) that meet within the ring, achieving their unity at the town's centre. The international sector, an area with a low density of population. causes little or no problem. In the industrial sector we plan extension space for each industry. Residential and cultural sectors are the most difficult to keep plastic and evolutive. At present, we still lack the financial means to build the macrostructure on which will be situated the more heavily populated part of the town. We shall then start with areas of lesser density.

By the way, all trees now on the site will be kept as they are.

Q: There have been talks about successive aspects of Auroville and even about many Aurovilles?

R.A.: We are now approaching the practical aspects of construction. After looking at Auroville as a whole, we must look at each aspect separately according to the growth of the town. Technically, with up to five thousand inhabitants we may utilize existing facilities, connect the power-lines to Neyveli's supply and use artesian wells for water. With a population of twenty five thousand, water problems become more acute in a district where water is scarce. We envisage then a sea-water desalinization plant. (This may not be the ultimate plant, as in the end Auroville will possess its own thermonuclear power unit). The same thing holds true for roads: we will make use of those now in existence up to the moment when the first deviations become necessary.

A first set of single-storied thatch-roofed polyhedric houses without foundation will allow, within six months, a grouping of ninety people around a small community building, a small shopping cente and a small maternity clinic where Auroville's first babies (two boys) have already been born. This organic unit will grow into another, three times bigger, which in turn will be integrated in a similar manner... each larger unit will be fitted with more and more cultural and sports installations. It may be that our first colony will not exceed one thousand persons. When we reach two or three thousand people, a first section of the future city will have been built. Our experimental colony may later become a part of Auroville or remain as an "historical site" or be completely rebuilt.

And so Auroville will have started, not unlike a big holiday village... to become ultimately one of South India's most important technical and cultural centres.

At a stage between five to ten thousand inhabitants we shall see what we call Auroville's first visage. Between ten and twenty-five thousand its second visage, and the third from twenty-five to fifty thousand. Above fifty thousand, new Aurovilles will start being built, let us hope, for Auroville is being devised to help solve community living problems all over the world.

Q: Would you like to take us on a science-fiction pre-visit to Auroville... by car...?

R.A.: ...to the residential sector. Huge parking areas await us, since no cars run within Auroville.

We first come to a zone of gardens and of private single-storey houses. It is a rather flat area, with widely diversified foliage, where houses are integrated with the terrain, by both color and building materials. Earth-coloured reddish tarmac lanes contribute to this cohesion. They meander up to the main ways.

As one goes deeper into this huge garden where pools scatter sunlight, one sees slightly higher houses, mostly two-storied, giving a striking impression of variety: no house is similar to another. Though their shapes are very audacious, they all retain a common look of simplicity, of tranquility. They open widely on very private patios. As we move forward, building materials

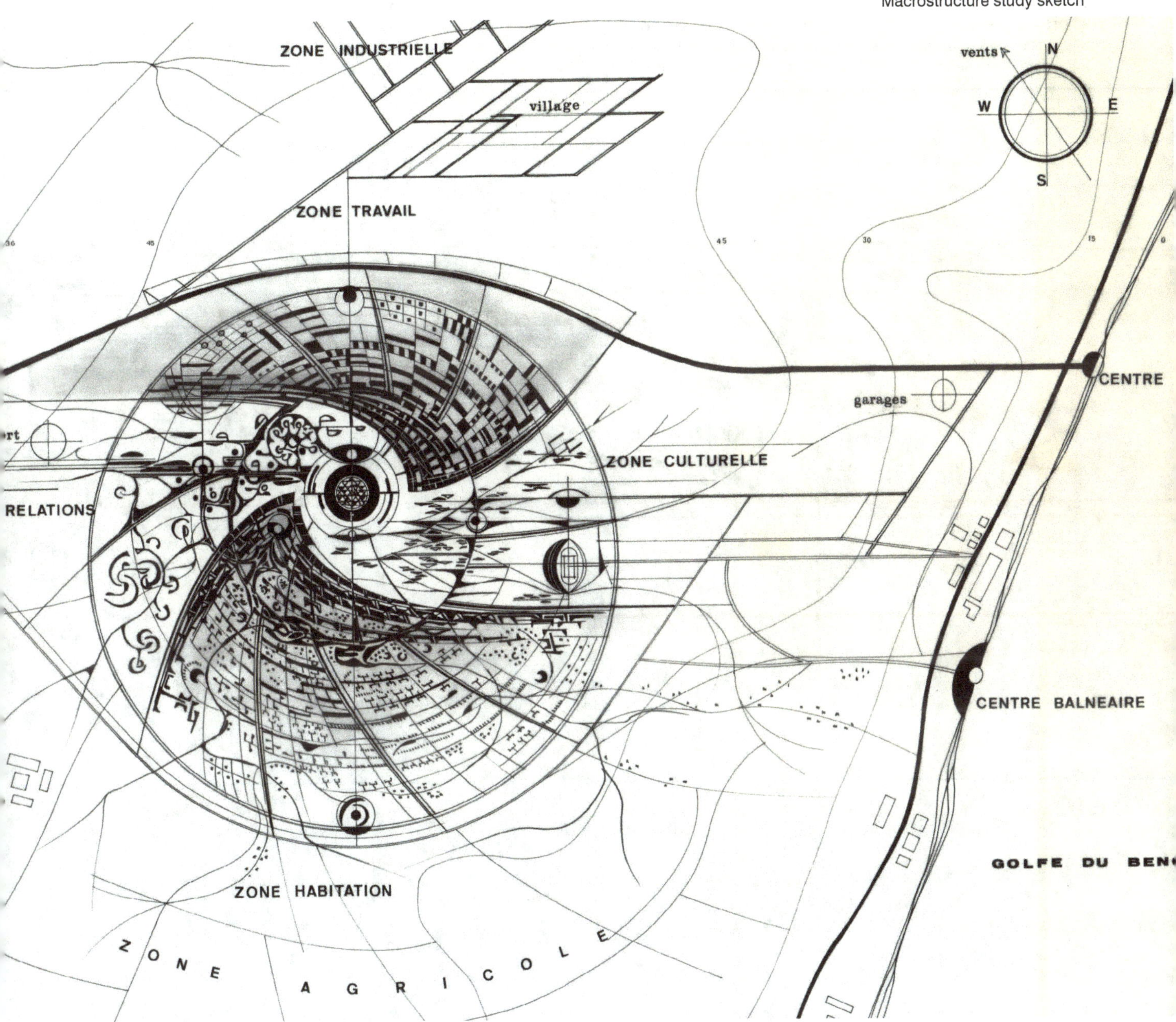
ZONE INDUSTRIELLE
village
ZONE TRAVAIL
vents
N
W
E
S
CENTRE
garages
ZONE CULTURELLE
RELATIONS
CENTRE BALNEAIRE
ZONE HABITATION
ZONE AGRICOLE
GOLFE DU BEN

and colours begin to shift according to a strange gradation, like a subtle rainbow weaving its own bridge of light and colours through the town.

Now lanes begin to look more like avenues or rather like mosaic-paved interconnections of a multiple building. None is straight but all lead to delightful fountains, squares, miniature multicolored arenas. It is a never-ending succession of discoveries and perspectives.

We are approaching the ring and the canal of the Great Curve where thousands of waterfowl play freely, and we go over one of the town's few bridges. As in a fairy-tale, we start climbing intriguing staircases rising and turning so softly and capriciously

against the sharp edges of great terraces that one may promenade for hours, contemplating all the faces of the town. Strolling along covered passages we discover handicraft makers and artists holding continual exhibitions; we play hide-and-seek with light and shadows, with activity and tranquility, stopping at last at the edge of a sculptured open space. At the foot of this regal balcony, on the inner side of the ring, stretches the Garden of Unity, encircling a shining lake whose running waters supply Auroville's canals, waterfalls, fountains and paddy-fields. From this lake rises a symbol of all manifestation, the intersection of all intersections, an unattainable white and golden island, burning like a high flame. This is the centre of Auroville, not a geometrical centre, but the core around which the ring gravitates in two waves, two helicoid movements trying to catch each other like

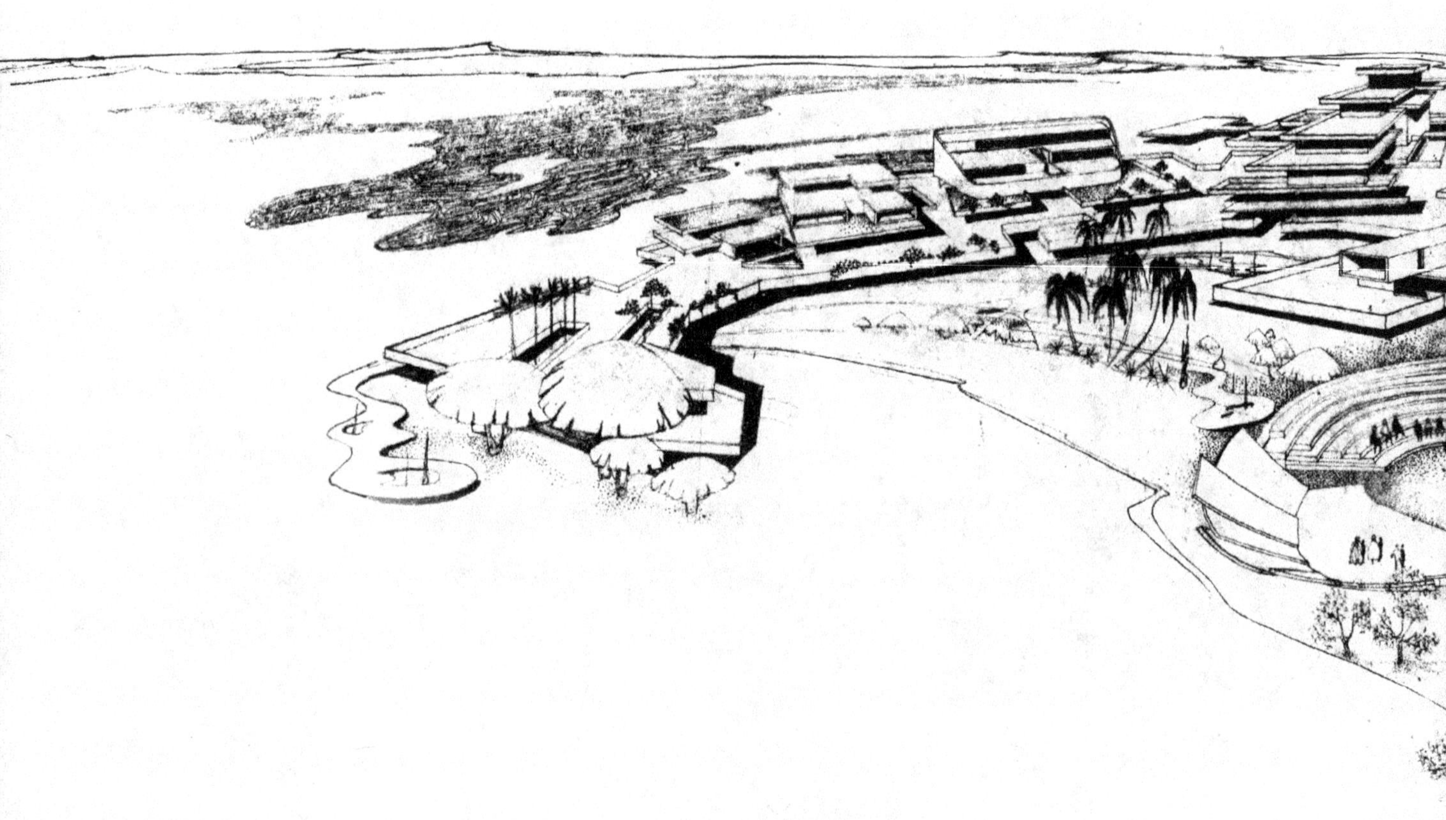

Yin and Yang, like two facing complementary galaxies, a symbol of Auroville's deepest dynamism.

Q: Two very beautiful symbols of Unity and the Two-in-One. Have you other symbols in Auroville?

R.A.: Water is for me a very powerful symbol. At rest, adorned with lotuses in pools, gliding along waterways, springing in fountains, coming alive with waterfalls, its presence is always a creation of force and beauty. I would like many waterways and pools in Auroville, though it may be quite an achievement in a country with such a water scarcity.

A specialist in our group is planning the creation of architectural forms giving birth to spherical plazas. A sphere is also a fine symbol. We are studying solar roofs that would allow each separate house to enjoy its own production of energy. Wouldn't it be a beautiful symbol of the global, solar consciousness that wants to manifest in Auroville?

But everything is a symbol in Auroville.

For us, the whole town and all its details are an expression of unity within diversity, the key not only to a happy architecture but to happy individuals, to a happy society, and finally to a happy planet.

Interview from Equals One, city, 1968

Proposal for Auromodel

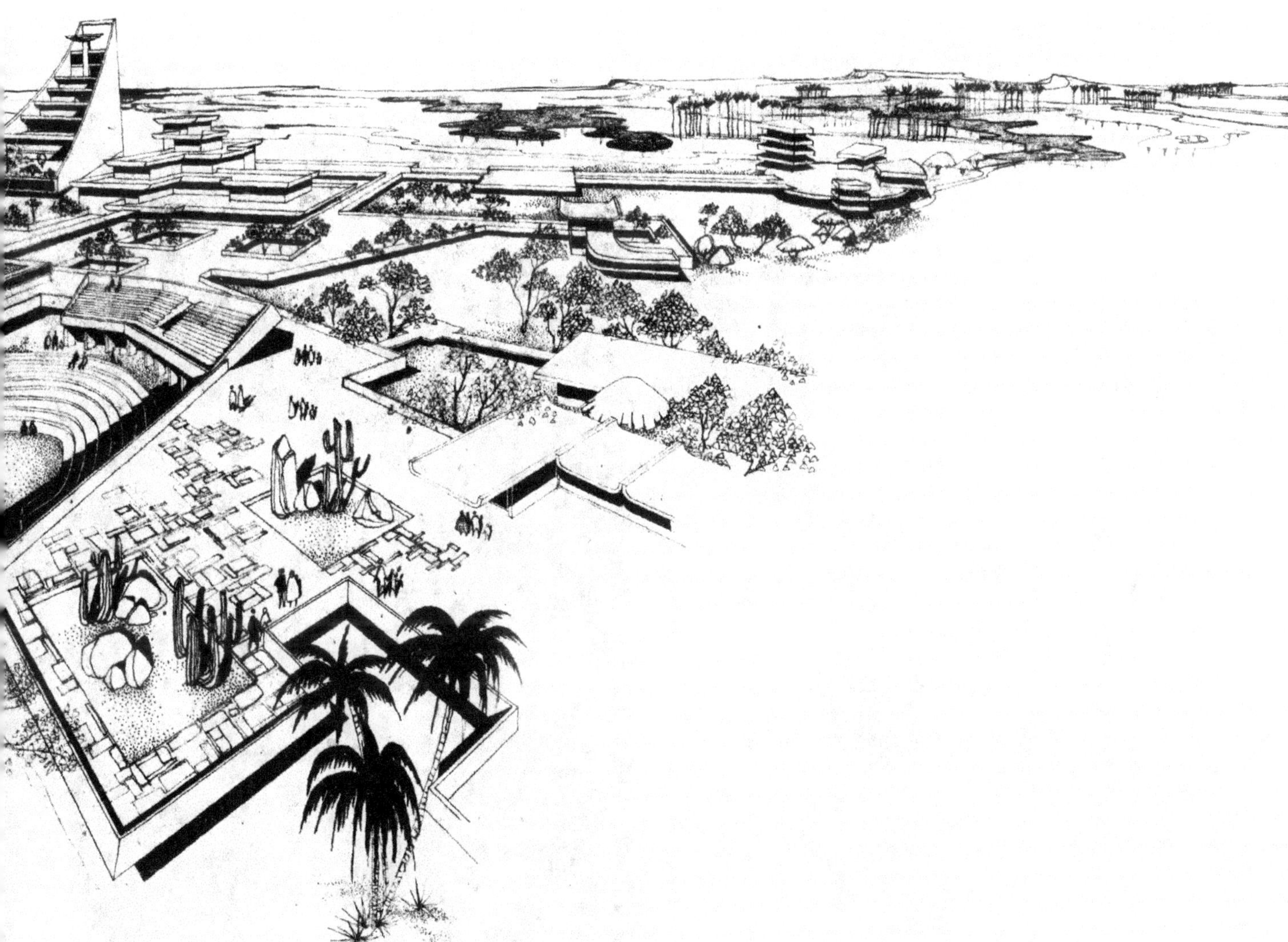

Early town planning

In 1965 Roger Anger, a practicing architect from Paris who had already been visiting Pondicherry regularly since 1956, was invited by the Mother to become the chief architect of Auroville. This challenge, which he readily accepted, engaged him passionately, commanding his special attention.

The plan for the city was that it would be realised through international participation and dedicated to achieving human unity. As chief architect, Roger Anger was given two important parameters: the figure of 50,000 inhabitants and four distinct zones to organise the principal activities of the city, accompanied by a hand-drawn sketch illustrating them. These were the residential, cultural, industrial and international zones. The international zone, unique to Auroville's proposed programme, was introduced in keeping with the importance of the international dimension and its necessary role in fulfilling Auroville's dedication to human unity. In close contact and extensive regular meetings with the Mother, detailed descriptions and directions were given to Roger Anger regarding the realisation of her vision of Auroville.

In March 1966, Roger Anger returned from Paris with two alternative proposals produced by his team there. The first was a rectangular grid plan, prepared by a team led by Puccinelli based on their Patio Homes project, with suspended gardens stacked in line with architecture produced in Paris and Grenoble.

The second, led by Heymann and Bratslavsky, was a symbolic and concentric plan with the city arranged around a strong central public space and twelve principal radial roads. Of the two proposals presented, the latter was dearly preferred, a plan that became known as the 'nebula' plan. However, the architect felt that the Mother was not entirely satisfied, as the plan appeared to lack something; he decided to try and make the city concept more dynamic.

Rectangular model, 1966
Hexagonal model, 1966 ▶

Hexagonal model, 1966
Nebula model, 1966

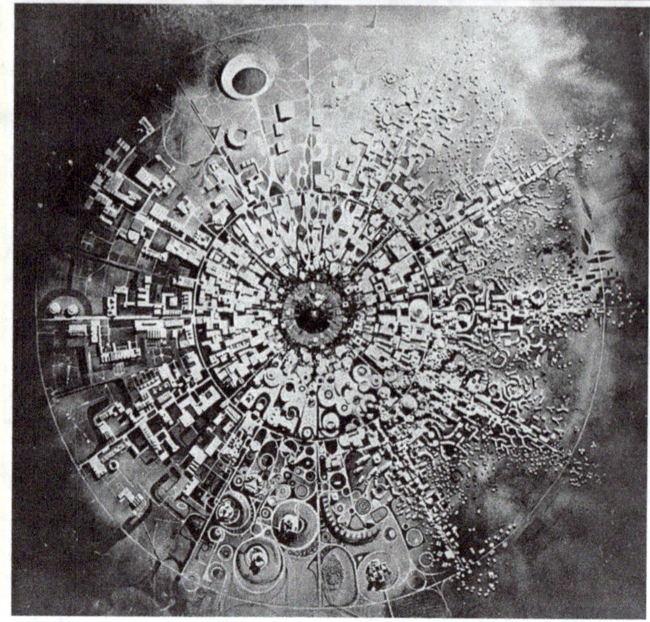

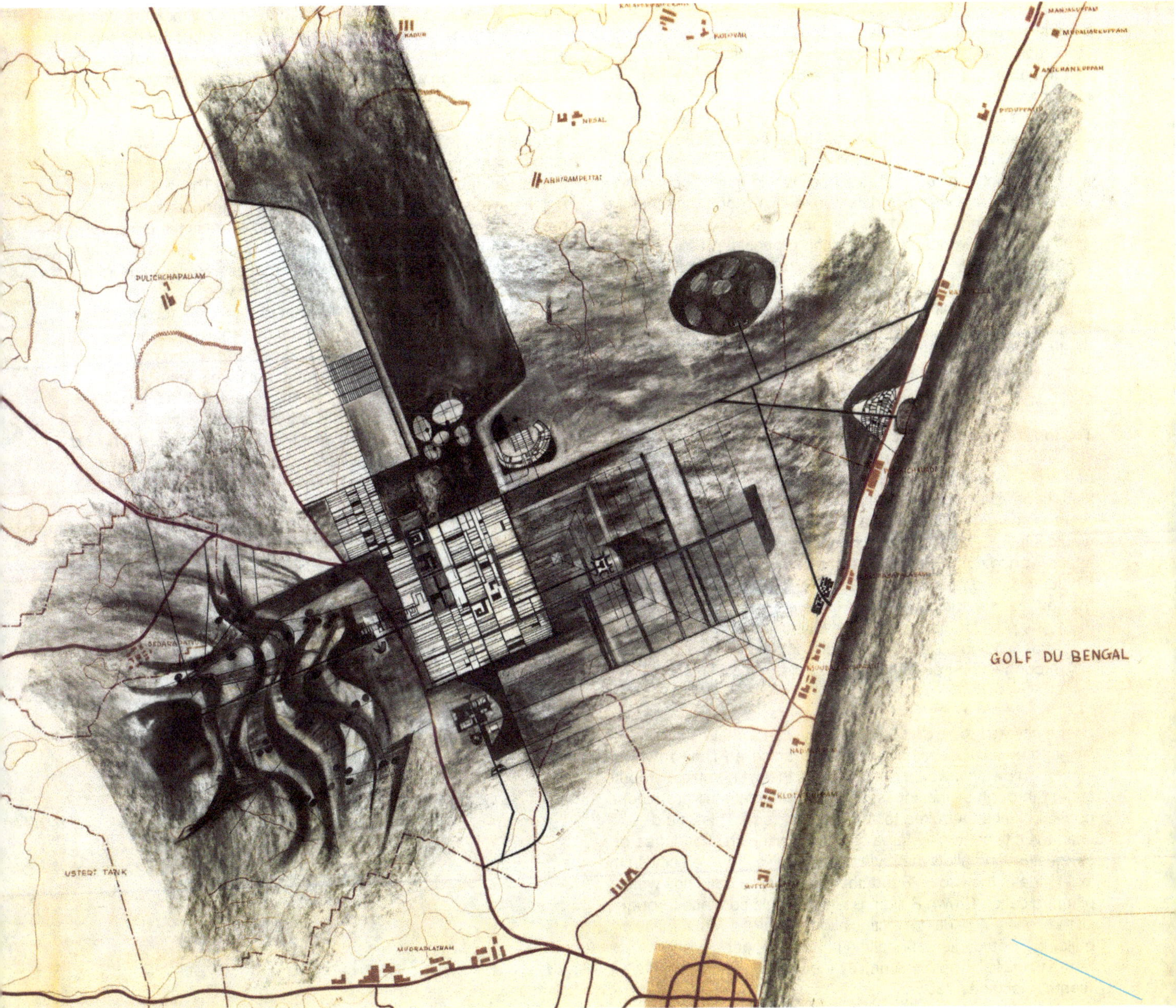

KADUR
KALASTRIPECCAM
KOTOVAR
MANJALKUPPAM
MUDALIARKUPPAM
ANICHANKUPPAM
NESAL
PIDUPPAKID
ARIHRAMPETTAI
PULICHCHAPALLAM
SEDARAPATU
GOLF DU BENGAL
NADUVARAI
KLOTAKUPPAM
MUTTUKAT
MUDRADLATNAM
USTERI TANK

In November 1967, the architect returned once again with a more dynamic adaptation of the concentric model into which a spiralling structure had been introduced. The residential and industrial zones which were denser than the international and cultural ones were marked with large macro-structures that reinforced the spiralling movement and were located opposite each other. This was felt too complex to be realised over time as the megastructures would have had to be built in more or less one sweep. The adoption of a more flexible concept seemed wiser. The fact that such tall structures would have blocked the view of the centre was also determined as a short-coming of the proposal. Having received this feedback, the design team in Paris continued their work and the resulting proposal, presented again in February 1968, just days before the formal inauguration event, was met with whole-hearted agreement. It has since continued to serve as the basis for Auroville's further development and planning. The attractive and dynamic city plan of powerful iconic quality was soon widely circulated and published; it came to symbolically represent the idea of Auroville itself.

The four zones were laid out in a dynamic radiating and spirally rotated movement around the city centre, consisting of a lake, parks and gardens. Anger explained that the zones were separated "only in theory," their gradual integration and communication facilitated by a circular plan. The rotation would allow the distinct zones to be less segregated, and to be interwoven to completely merge at the city centre as a unified whole. Initially a massive sculpture of a flame was planned at the very centre, surrounded by a large artificial circular lake. By 1971, the plan for the centre had evolved into an oval island with a central building called Matrimandir representing the soul of this city. A congestion-free city centre was desired and planned.

As the city was to be so compact, only 2.5 kilometres in diameter, it was to be serviced via a concentric road called The Crown, located midway; it would both serve as the main traffic distributor, cutting through all the zones, and accommodate the prominent public buildings required to service each zone. This would keep the city centre, the area contained within this road, free of congestion and allow the town to remain like a garden city. In the inner side of the Crown Road, the main service buildings were planned called Crown Buildings which would continue through all the zones. A pedestrian circulation contained within these buildings would interconnect them. Roger Anger envisaged "a bustling life", within this ring as the vital soul of the city, its "centripetal focus. "80

A green belt was planned to surround the city and absorb its impact. In order to achieve the desired density without reducing its contact to nature, and in order to achieve about 50% green areas, the bulk of the city structure would largely be composed of low-rise buildings with some concentrated macrostructures.

Although it didn't originate from the architects themselves, this plan became popularly known as the' galaxy' plan due to the formal resemblance between the two images. This has led to a general misconception of the architect's intent, as having deliberately applied the spiralling form to express the universal nature of the project. The formal aspect was therefore considered to have been overrated in the design process. However, Roger Anger asserted that this version of the plan was the result of an ongoing architectural process that began when the founder preferred the direction of a concentric development over a grid-shaped one. Thereafter, the final design was the product of a natural evolution of the work carried out by his team on that basis. This is evident from the interim presentation model with the mega structures. Anger does admit though that with the inauguration approaching, it was a truly inspired expression, and that there was a certain conviction about it among the team of architects who were working on that version of the design. Anger clarified that he first heard the term 'galaxy' related to the city plan much later when 'The Mother' informed him of an American disciple who had brought a NASA photograph of the galaxy that had been released, and had discussed the resemblance of it with Auroville's city plan.

In 1968, the planned city was inaugurated on a 'wasteland' with the support of UNESCO and the participation of people from 124 countries, who each brought a handful of earth from their homelands to a marble-clad lotus bud-shaped urn that now stands at its centre.

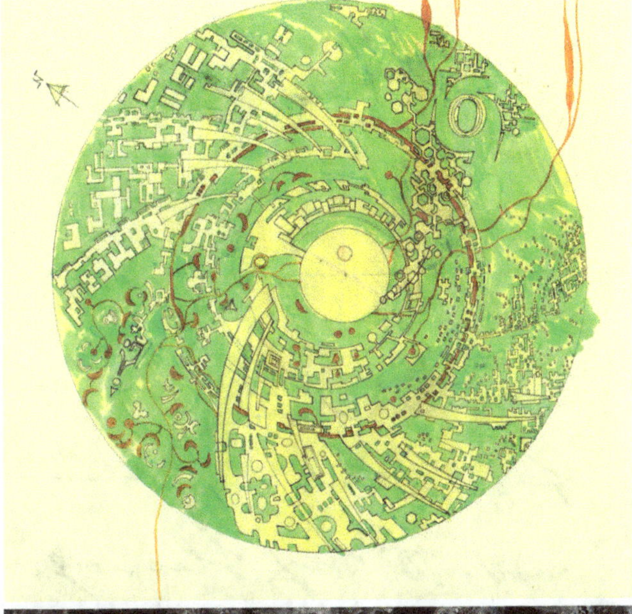

Galaxy plan study sketch

The Galaxy Model was presented to the Mother for approval by Roger Anger early in 1968 and was subsequently presented at the inauguration of Auroville on 28 February 1968.

Galaxy model, 1968

Auromodéle was conceived as a settlement of 2,000 inhabitants. It was planned in the early stages of Auroville's development, deliberately outside the city area and eastward towards the Bay of Bengal, as the first living experiment to be undertaken in the creation of the city.

As the name implies, this settlement was to serve as a model for the city and to be a playing field, a laboratory for trial and error and concrete experimentation towards discovering the nature of the collective life that could be expected within the ideal city. It was to facilitate the necessary mistakes and allow their evaluation in an area outside the planned city, where lands had yet to be consolidated.

Data about the emerging international community life could be obtained from here and used to detail the city proper. This approach would relieve the pressure to develop the final city infrastructure immediately and allow life in Auroville to emerge while providing the residents who were already arriving there with housing on Auroville land before the city was ready.

Auromodéle was planned adjacent to another temporary housing cluster for fresh arrivals called Aspiration, and various related facilities for everyday life were located there such as a school campus, a grocery store, the State Bank of India, and some manufacturing units.

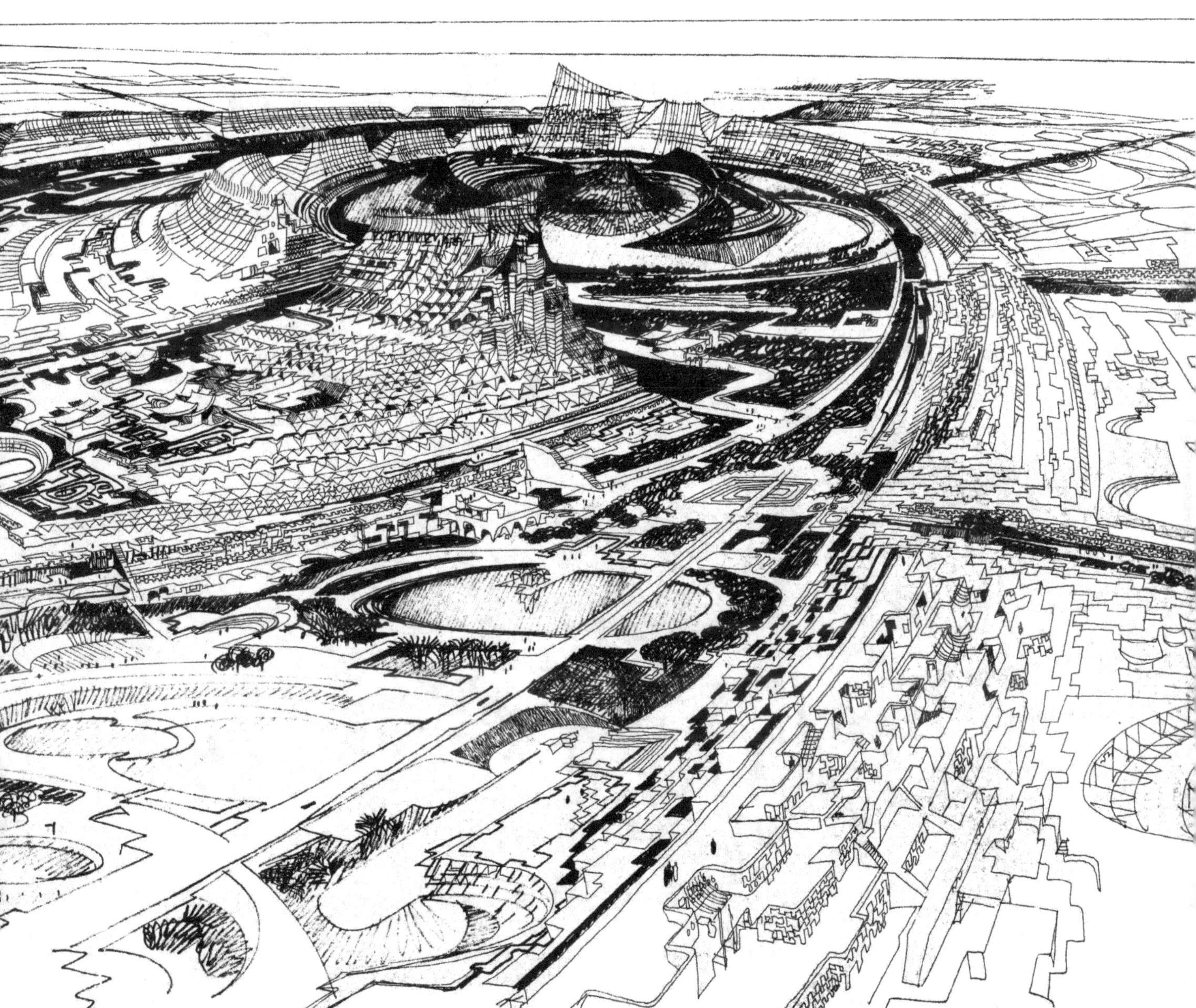

The Lines of Force enhance the dynamic spiraling movement
of the town plan, absorb density with a minimum of circulation
on the ground through vertical development, and provide vistas
and views of the city itself from various viewpoints that would
otherwise not be visible in this relatively flat land.

View / sketch

The Lines of Force are one of the most important features of
the Galaxy Plan and play a central role in defining the 'dynamic
movement' of this plan form. The Lines of Force create a 'hill
like' ambiance in the city area, at the same time providing the
possibility of compact development, to optimise the use of land
while providing efficient service infrastructure. This compact
development ensures that the remainder of the land can be
developed more as open space.

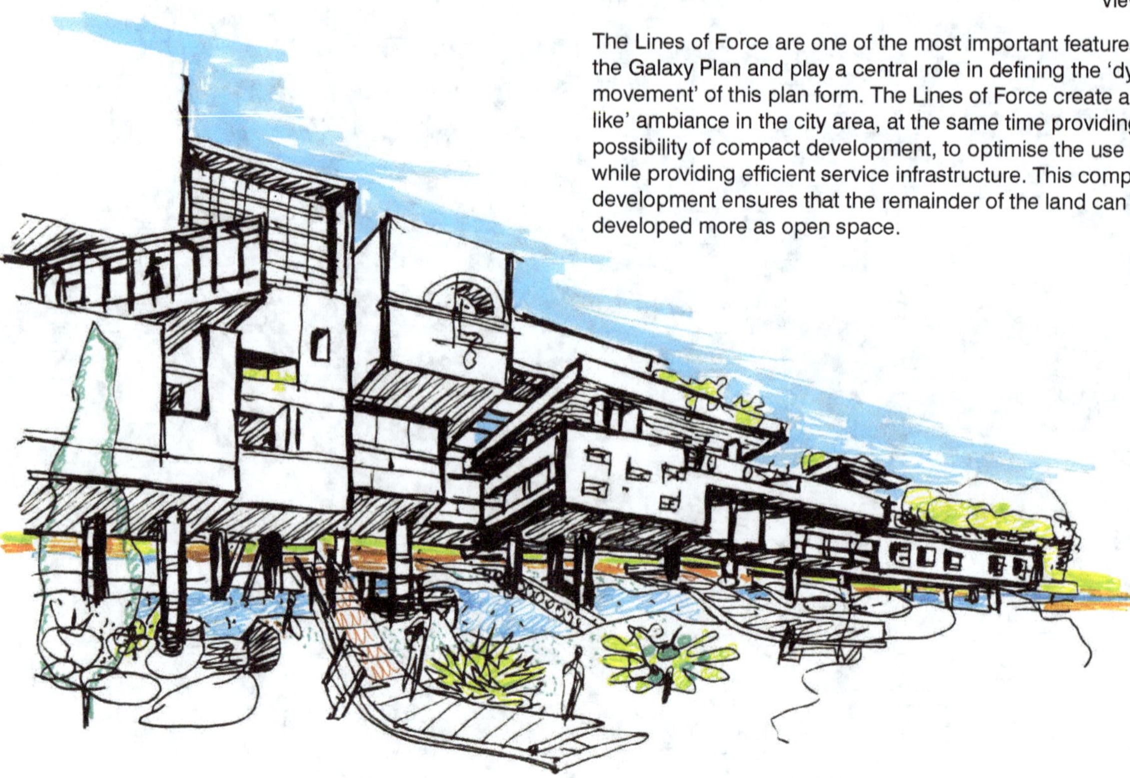

Sketch showing flow of open spaces under the building.

Croquis de principe montrant la pénétration sous le bâtiment

The four zones were laid out in a dynamic radiating and spirally rotated movement around the city centre, inclusive of a lake, parks and gardens. Roger Anger explained that the zones were separated "only in theory," their gradual integration and communication facilitated by a circular plan. The rotation would allow the distinct zones to be less segregated, and to be interwoven to completely merge at the city centre as a unified whole.

As the city was to be so compact, only 2.5 kms in diameter, it was to be serviced via a concentric road called The Crown, located midway between the centre and perimeter; it would both serve as the main traffic distributor, cutting through all the zones, and accommodate the prominent public buildings required to service each zone.

This would keep the city centre, the area contained within this road, free of congestion and allow the town to remain like a garden city. In the inner side of the Crown Road, the main service buildings were planned called Crown Buildings, which would continue through all the zones. A pedestrian circulation contained within these buildings would interconnect them. Roger Anger envisaged "a bustling life" within this ring as the vital soul of the city, its 'centripetal focus.'

Text extracted from the book "Roger Anger, Research on Beauty, Recherche sur la beauté, Architecture 1953-2008", by Anupama Kundoo, Jovis Verlag publishers

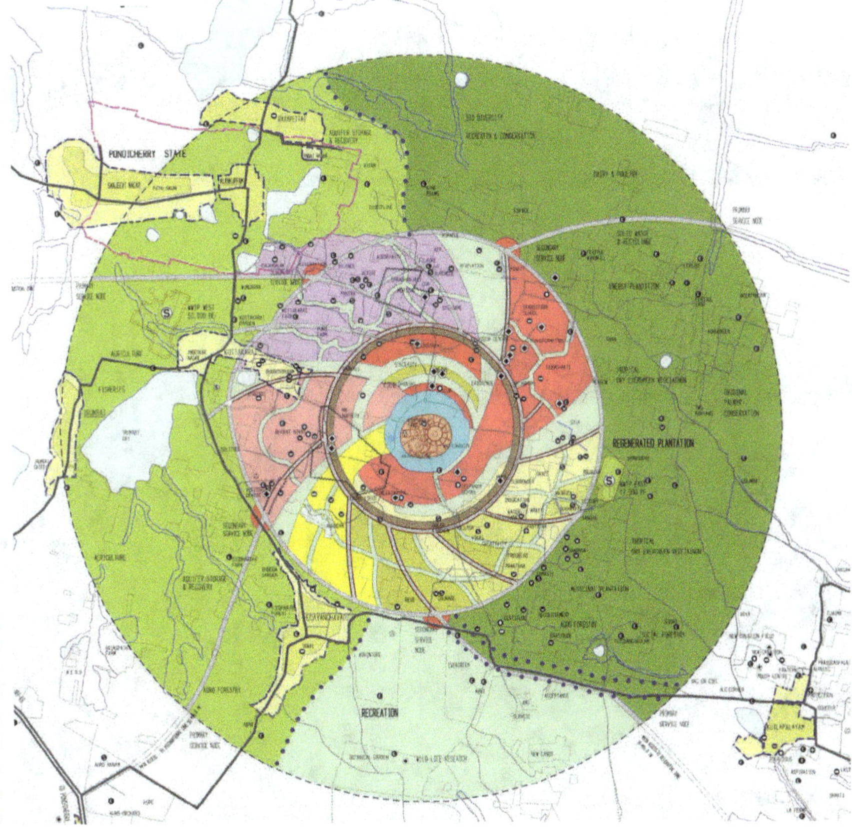

Mother's original sketch of the four zones

Auroville Master Plan - proposed land use
plan, 2001
The four zones of Auroville
International zone
Cultural zone
Residential zone
Industrial zone
Green Belt

Early
Aspiration
settlement

Architects: Piero & Gloria Cicionesi, 1969

Foundation stone of Last School being laid by Aurofilio on 13-4-1970

Construction of Last School, 1971   Architect: Roger Anger   Pyramid School under construction

Construction work at Last School

Typical casuarina structure for a ▶
building, prior to being thatched

Construction work at Auromodèle

Early creative and experimental architecture

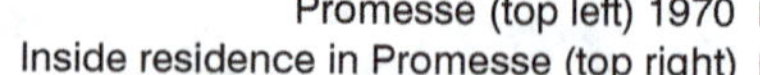

Promesse (top left) 1970 ▶
Inside residence in Promesse (top right) ▶

Experimental sphere-shaped house in ▶
Forecomers settlement (bottom left and right)

Forecomers 1969

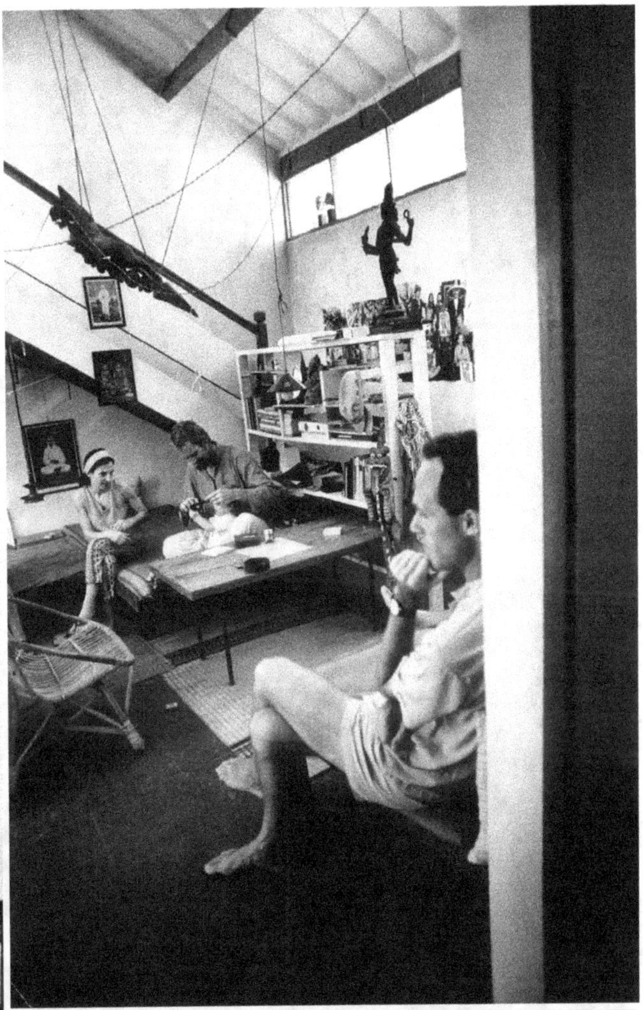

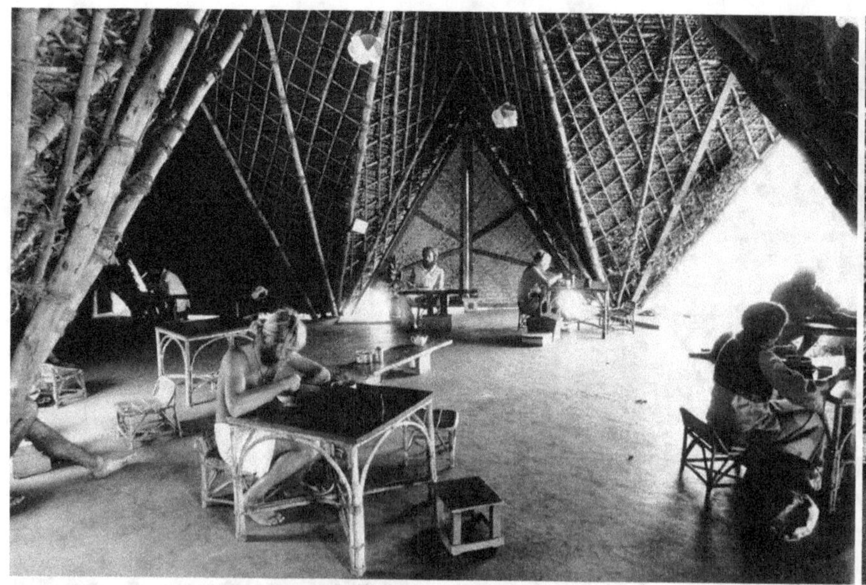

Community kitchen at Protection settlement, in the 1970s

Canyon house in Forecomers, 1972

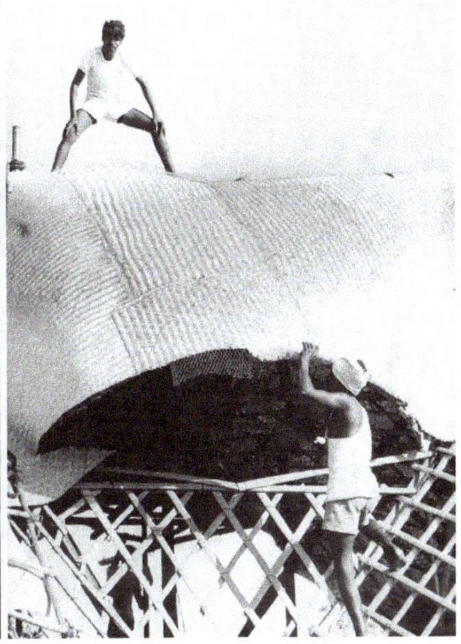

Artist: Rolf Lieser

House in Ami... a world of flowing Daliesque-like forms, a whisper of surrealism sited among the cashew fields.

"We built it in 1985 very fast. I did the drawings in two weeks, and the third week we started digging the foundations. In five months it was finished. After living under keet for some time, I'd had enough of the dirt. So in this house, the roof is a mixture of vermiculite, sand and cement laid over bamboo matting and strips of pakkumaram wood, all supported on granite pillars. The walls – which are separate from the roof structure – are brick, the windows ferro-cement."

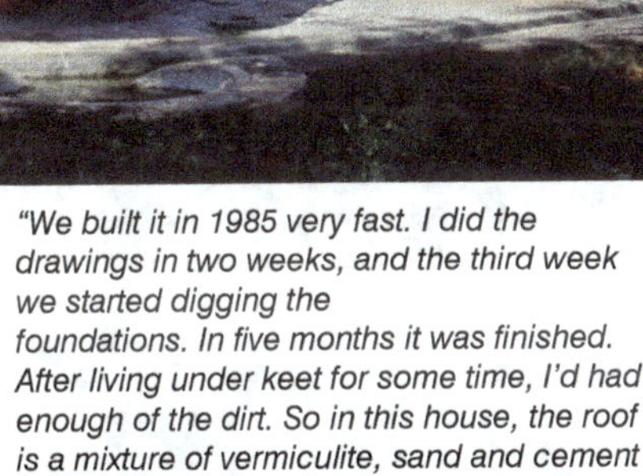

House in Samriddhi settlement

Tent house in Fraternity, 1975

44

The Soul of the City

Clockwise from top left:
Excavation work, 10.50 metres deep and 50 metres across at ground level from 1971-1972

The Mothers 94th birthday meditation, 21st February 1972

Matrimandir construction in 1979
Dawn bonfire at Auroville's Amphitheatre in 2007

Architect: Roger Anger

At the very centre of Auroville one finds the Matrimandir, a huge gold disc-clad sphere, which seems to be rising out of the earth, symbolising the birth of a new consciousness.

The Mother described it as the "symbol of the Divine's answer to man's aspiration for perfection", and as "the central cohesive Force" of Auroville.

It is situated in a large open area called 'Peace', which is planned to be the site of beautifully landscaped gardens creating different atmospheres, from where the evolving township begins to radiate outwards.

The atmosphere within and around the Matrimandir is quiet and charged, and the area naturally beautiful, even though at present large parts of it are still under construction/development.

Literally 'Temple of the Mother' (though it is not in fact a temple), located at the heart of the township, the Matrimandir is seen as the "soul of Auroville".

It contains an all-white marble-clad Inner Chamber with white carpet, where a beam of light focuses down onto a 70 cm diameter optical quality glass globe surrounded by 12 white pillars.

The Matrimandir will be the soul of Auroville. The sooner the soul is there, the better it will be for everybody and especially for the Aurovilians.

A place...for trying to find one's consciousness.

*It is like the Force,
the central Force of Auroville,
the cohesive Force of Auroville.*

- The Mother

Contact:
Matrimandir
605101 Auroville, Tamil Nadu - INDIA
Tel: 0413-262-2204, 262-2268
matrimandir@auroville.org.in

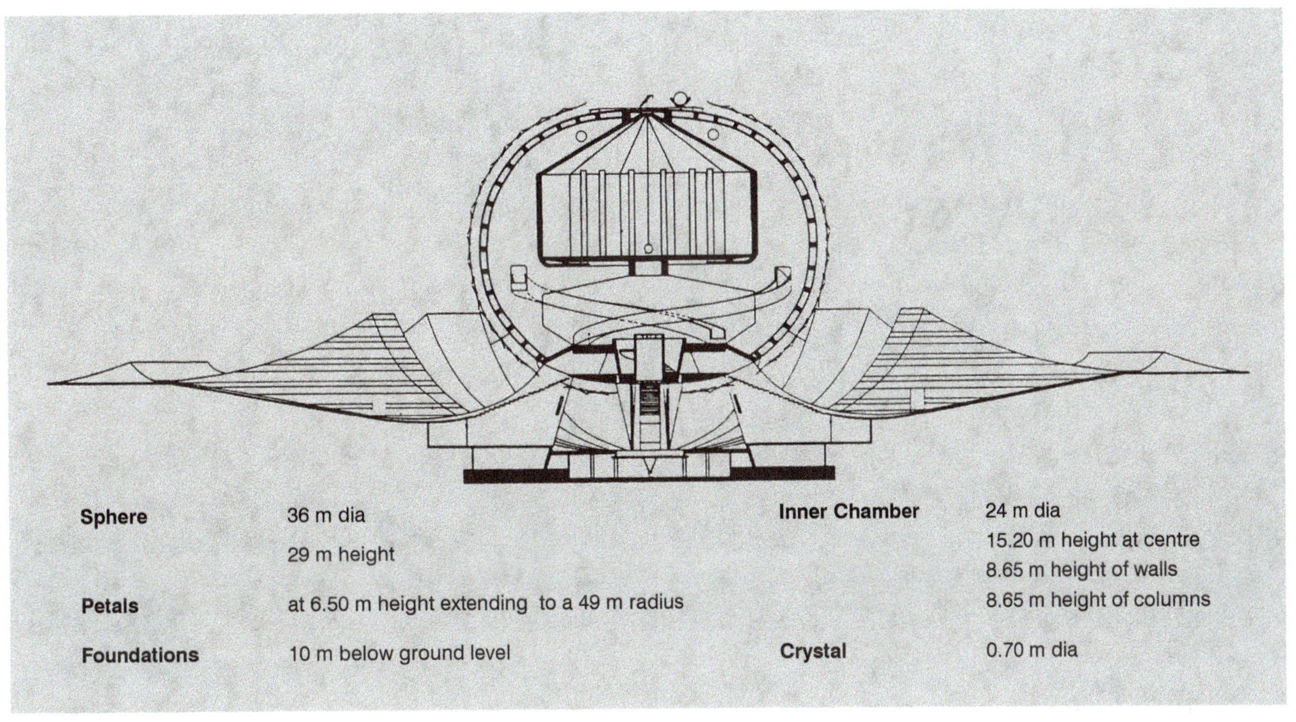

Sphere	36 m dia	**Inner Chamber**	24 m dia
	29 m height		15.20 m height at centre
			8.65 m height of walls
Petals	at 6.50 m height extending to a 49 m radius		8.65 m height of columns
Foundations	10 m below ground level	**Crystal**	0.70 m dia

Matrimandir area

Gardens

1 Existence
2 Consciousness
3 Bliss
4 Light
5 Life
6 Power
7 Wealth
8 Utility
9 Progress
10 Youth
11 Harmony
12 Perfection

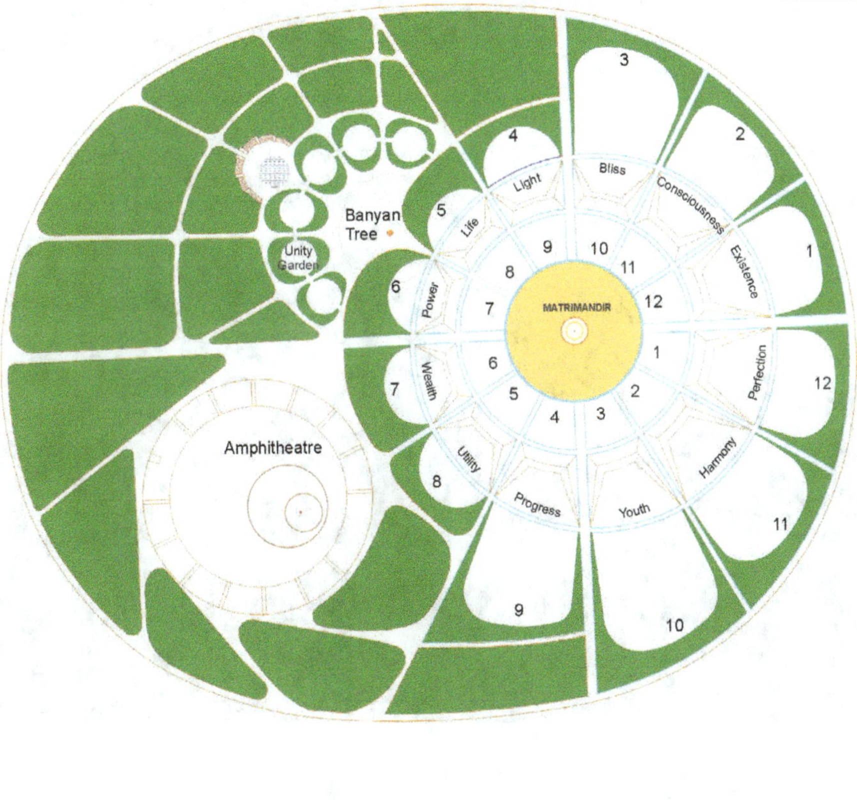

Meditation rooms

1 Sincerity
2 Humility
3 Gratitude
4 Perseverance
5 Aspiration
6 Receptivity
7 Progress
8 Courage
9 Goodness
10 Generosity
11 Equality
12 Peace

Banyan Tree
Geographical Centre
of Auroville

View of the base of the two ramps and Mother's symbol

Inner Chamber

There are no images, no organised meditations, no flowers, no incense, no religions or religious forms. It is a place, in the Mother's words, for *"those who want to learn to concentrate.*

No fixed meditations, none of all that, but they should stay there in silence, in silence and concentration.
A place for trying to find one's consciousness."

North entrance to the Matrimandir

Marble entrance to the stairs leading to the second level

Marble lotus pond below the Matrimandir

The Petals
Surrounding the central sphere there are twelve "petals", each planned to contain a meditation chamber with a different interior finish designed to create 12 different environments for meditation.

The 70-cm optically perfect glass globe at the heart of the Matrimandir's Inner Chamber is illuminated by a focused beam of light from above.

Amphitheatre

Located adjacent to the Matrimandir and central banyan tree at the heart of Auroville, the Amphitheatre has as its focal point a marble-clad urn containing soil placed by representatives of the 124 nations and 23 Indian States that participated in the 1968 Auroville inauguration ceremony.

Today the Amphitheatre is used as a place for pre-dawn bonfires which draw Aurovilians and friends of Auroville together on New Year's morning, Auroville's birthday (Feb 28) and Sri Aurobindo's birthday (Aug 15), and for gatherings conducive to the raising of consciousness and "inward" focus. It also houses the control room and machinery for the Matrimandir electrical, air-conditioning and communication systems.

Architect: Roger Anger

Research in architecture

Auroville wants to be a field of constant research for architectural expressions, manifesting a new spirit through new forms.

- The Mother

A spirit of experimentation and a search for new ways of being in all aspects of life, both individual and collective, are part of Auroville's very "raison d'etre". As such, architecture in Auroville aims at promoting research, experimentation, creativity and harmony, as well as functionally integrated development.

This spirit, along with a commitment to address socio-economic and environmental concerns, underlies much of what is being attempted in the fields of design and architecture in Auroville. Its goal is to be in harmony with nature, and to follow a sustainable model taking into account the prevalent climatic and sociological conditions of the region.

In addition, Auroville is also intensively involved in technology transfer through workshops, student exchange and intern programmes, presentations and seminars. Through these activities it reaches out to a multitude of people and diverse municipalities, from remote rural areas in India to developed cities worldwide.

Pioneering years
Since its inception, the possibility of creating a city within this "ideal-seeking" environment has attracted large numbers of architects, planners, students and researchers.

The pioneering years saw the construction of very simple, self-designed – and sometimes self-built – huts of casuarina poles and palm thatch; the start of the Matrimandir and some school buildings; the early construction of the Pavilion of India (the Bharat Nivas complex); and the first experiments in community living in 'Aspiration' and 'Auromodèle'.

In the difficult period of the 1960 and 70s, when adequate financial and human resources were lacking, the limited availability of construction materials provoked a creative revolution among the self-builders. Structures were taken to high levels of self expression and imagination, some of which remain as amazing architectural expositions of form that break conventional moulds.

Present trends
Today's Auroville contains a wide range of dwellings from single to collective housing. These, plus a considerable number of educational, institutional and public buildings, represent the bulk of Auroville's development over the past two decades.

Looking to the future, present experiments cover various aspects of architecture, which include appropriate building materials and technologies such as ferrocement and compressed earth blocks, eco-friendly climate-responsive designs able to protect against heat, dust, sound intrusion, monsoon rain and cyclonic winds, integration with natural surroundings, cost-effective buildings, geomancy and geometry, security against theft and the intrusions of ants, termites and other creatures, and the design of space itself. Lifestyle and its impact on design and management of building infrastructure, integrated rainwater harvesting systems, domestic wastewater treatment plants, and the integration of solar power systems are presently rich fields of research and experimentation.

From thatch and bamboo houses in the past to reinforced concrete structures, from single standing residences to apartment complexes and public buildings, Auroville remains a research field for expressing an ever-expanding variety of architectural forms.

Meeting of L'avenir d'Auroville group

Planning the township

One of the most remarkable concepts of Auroville is its original conceptual design as a township, laid out in the form of a galaxy - a galaxy in which several 'arms' seem to unwind from a central area. In interviews with Auroville Today in 1988 and 1992, Roger Anger explained how this plan came into existence:

"Mother had given a couple of parameters: the division of the city into four areas, or zones, and the number of people for whom the city is envisaged (50,000). The division into those four zones (industrial, residential, international and cultural) is unique, and has no precedent in town planning. On the basis of this scheme, we, the architects and town planners, started to make suggestions to her. This was done in several stages, and finally the Galaxy came out and was presented as a model to Mother, and accepted by her as a plan that answered to her parameters. She inspired and guided the work. When I talked to Mother one day about Auroville, she said that the city already exists on a subtle level, that it is already constructed, that it is only necessary to pull it down, to make it descend on earth."

The galaxy plan shows the four zones, which are interconnected through the 'Crown', the second circular road around the Matrimandir. From the Crown, twelve roads radiate outwards as part as the infrastructure. Some of them are accompanied by a succession of high-rise buildings, which constitute the so-called 'Lines of Force', essential for the framework of the city and for the integration of all access to the city centre. But the plan is not finished. On the contrary, the city is still to be invented, everything has still to be done through the daily experience and rhythm of the Aurovilians. Apart from these lines of force, everything is flexible, nothing is fixed."*

- Roger Anger

Map shows a non-finalized City Area, 2010

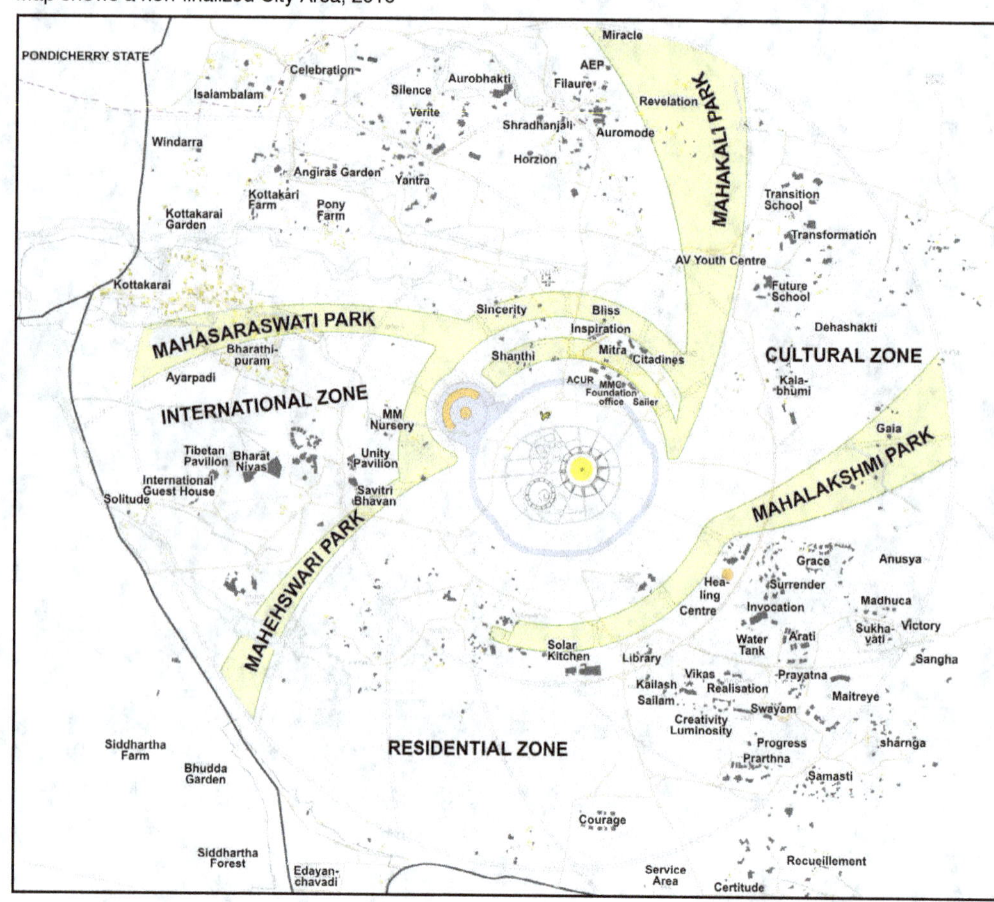

Through its Master Plan, Auroville wants to break new ground in settlement-planning in such a way as to help other cities, both in India and abroad, which are experiencing high urbanisation trends. Auroville also hopes to demonstrate how 'urban' & 'rural' areas can complementarily develop in an integral and holistic way for their mutual benefit and well-being.

Location of the four zones

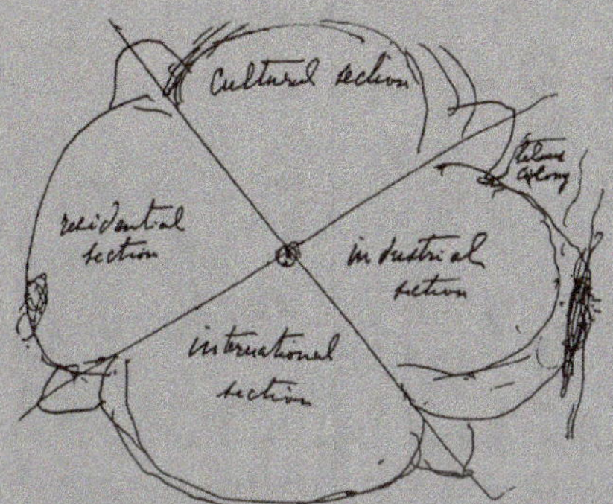

Mother's original sketch of the four zones

We have four big sections: the cultural section, to the north, that is to say, towards Madras; to the east, the industrial section; to the south, the international section; and to the west, that is to say towards the lake, the residential section. ...This industrial section is to the east and it is very big, there is plenty of space; it will go down towards the sea and if possible, there would be a kind of wharf, not exactly a port but a place where boats could come alongside...

I have no illusions that it [the concept] will keep its original purity, but we shall try something.

- Mother on 23 June 1965, speaking about Auroville for the first time.

Features of the township

The Auroville area, which extends over 20 sq.kms, has two identifiable parts — the City, which is distinctly urban and is 5 sq. kms. in extent, and the Green Belt, 15 sq. kms in extent.

The City area is comprised of four zones — the Residential, Industrial, International and Cultural – each with its specific use, centred around the Peace area which contains the Matrimandir, the Amphitheatre and the Banyan Tree. The Green Belt, where some village settlements are also located, consists of areas of farming, regenerated forest, and areas for recreation and other non-urban uses, and will be a rich laboratory for sustainable development practices.

The population of Auroville will consist of peoples of all nationalities, voluntarily attracted to the township to serve humanity. It is designed to eventually accommodate up to 50,000 residents, the majority of whom will live in the Residential Zone of 427 acres. The Master Plan envisages a phased development, with a population of 10–15,000 by 2010. The projected final density of the Residential Zone is 100 people per acre.

The township's design is eminently suited to cost-effective decentralised systems in terms of water supply, waste treatment and recycling. Auroville's goal in terms of energy is to become entirely independent through the development of alternative sources, though up to now it has continued to draw much of its energy from the grid. The road system has been designed to encourage use by non-polluting traffic. A network of cycle and pedestrian paths is envisaged in the green corridors within the city area.

The Auroville Development Plan envisages massive investment spread over the different zones to enable Auroville to reach its full potential progressively and rapidly. This will also help Auroville extend the benefits of its development to the surrounding villages and bioregion.

The Development Plan is complemented by a set of zoning regulations that will help Auroville to develop and channel all land usage within 20 square kilometres into planned and desirable directions. The Plan has also identified an organisational set-up that will assist the process of plan preparation and implementation to achieve the goals, objectives and vision in the establishment of the township.

(from the Master Plan)

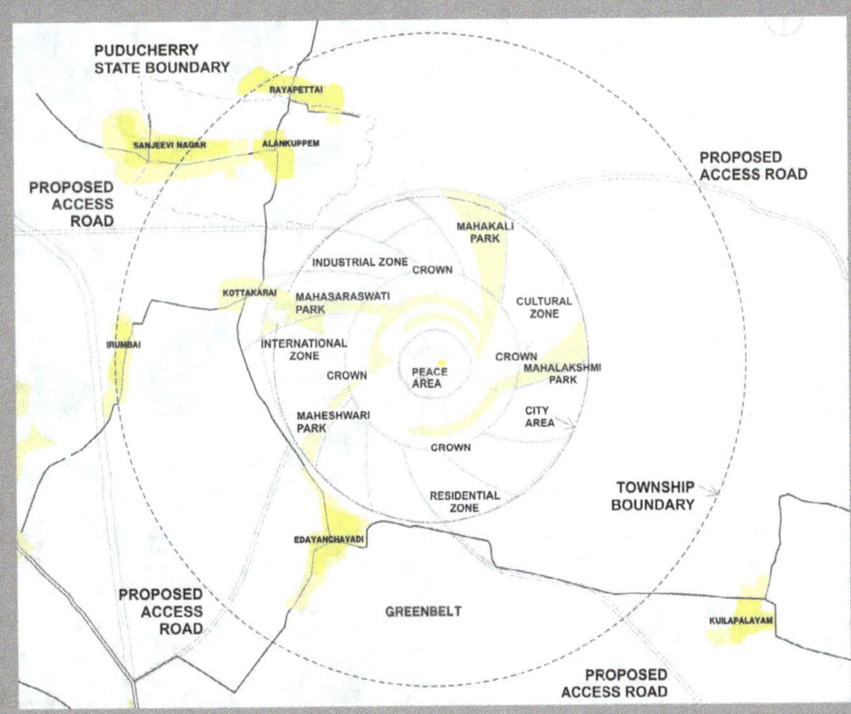

Decoding the Galaxy

Study the galaxy plan, and it's easy to be moved by its beauty, yet over the years we have been drifting away from it. This has lead to a fear that unless we do something drastic we could find ourselves in a chaotic urban sprawl like any other little town around Auroville, like Tindivanam or Villupuram for example. The question therefore arises, what can we do to correct the present trend?

My practical re-involvement with the city's growth has been quite recent, only since around 2008, when I started to work with two Auroville architects on 'Progress', the Line of Force started by Dominic years ago. We had wonderful brainstorming sessions where we tried to put into practice some visions from the Dreamcatcher meetings.

The recurrent leitmotiv in these sessions was to find a language where architecture, art and ecology could join to make a truly new urban way of living, embodying the Auroville ideal.

At one point both architects dropped out of the sessions due to heavy work pressure. Left alone, I continued making models, and after many attempts I found a very fluid and dynamic way of making models of the Line of Force, and I eventually ended up with a 1/1000 model of the whole galaxy.

It was beautiful, like a dream, a vision of the future, but looking at it every day I progressively got scared and frustrated. Scared, because the jump from where we are now to what these megastructures represented I found just too big even for our boldest imagination. Frustrated, because once more we would be confronted with a concept which we have absolutely no way of entering or manifesting. It seemed to be an all-or-nothing situation where unless we got a massive grant from Bill Gates or Santa Claus, we would be back to capsules and channel-roof buildings.

Then one day I started looking at another challenge: how to connect these buildings, and I saw what there was from the beginning, in the Galaxy model, a double spiral movement. First a clockwise movement that we all know, made by the Lines of Force, but also a second anti-clockwise movement implied in the dynamism of the Residential Zone.

Then came the 'eureka' moment. I was working on the big 1/1000 model with thermocool; I had with me a portion of the big circle corresponding to the 'outer circle' of the city. I found that by translating this circle tangentially around the crown I was

very close to the implied movement I had seen.

By putting these two movements together, I came to the grid visible in the picture.

The grid remained for some time on my

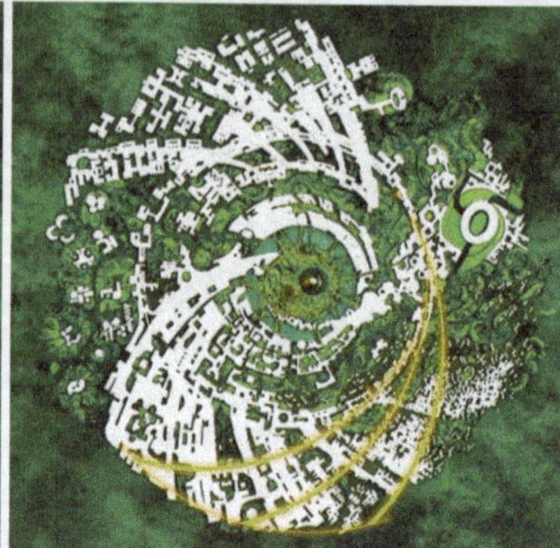

table, until I realized its full potential;
so much so that it became much more
important than the buildings.

Why?
As I mentioned earlier, thinking of the
buildings is frustrating, because:

1st - we don't have the means to start even
the smallest of these megastructures

2nd - we don't have the skill here, or the gift,
to attempt such a huge leap.

I remembered suddenly a book I had
seen many years ago, which described
the evolution of famous cities: Florence,
Istanbul, etc, and what fascinated me was
the fact that in a town the most permanent
feature is not the buildings (the built space),
but the streets, the plazas, the water bodies,
etc (the not-built-on spaces).

So to come back to my fear of finding
ourselves in a faceless urban sprawl due
to our haphazard and piecemeal growth,
justified by our lack of means, we had here
a solution: let us put in place the not-built-on
spaces first, in such a way that we keep the
main feature of the Galaxy - its dynamism.

Then we are safe.

Because, whatever we do, our city will retain
the original dynamism. And if we follow its
dynamism our buildings will progressively
attain the quality, the originality and the
'newness' that the Mother envisioned.

For that we need lesser means.

Practically, there are many ways to interpret
this grid and put it in place.

First, it could remain virtual, a set of lines on
the plan that we respect whenever we are
faced with a new project.

The grid could be traced on the ground
as mud roads or paths, so that we are
constantly aware of the dynamism of our
future city.

Progressively, some portions of these axis
roads could be paved, according to need.

Some of these roads could be temporary, for
transporting building materials, for instance,
and could then be cancelled afterwards to
give space for parks, etc.

Some of these lines could only be 'service
corridors' where we could put in place the
water lines, electric lines, etc.

Some could be lines of trees.

We could also study the density of this grid.

On the one hand it could be very wide, so as
to leave plenty of space for a more informal
growth.

In some places it could remain very dense,
so as to allow some parameters for the
orientation of the buildings.

When we have a dense grid, we can also
imagine giving height parameters, so that
we can also achieve the vertical dynamism
of the Lines of Force.

We speak of a grid. But perhaps we should
also speak of the in-between plots. This
opens a new range of possibilities for an
organic growth: we could, for example, give
a full plot to an architect to develop, along
with a few parameters, allowing us to move
from one finished section to another finished
section.

Also, we can think of doing this only now,
as the major portion of the land is available.
Until now, most projects had to follow the
boundary of the bought land, which also
explains the haphazard growth. Now we
have to start looking at the whole territory as
one single entity.

Because of the grid, we can still build in a
piecemeal way, and yet because of it we can
also hold the vision of the total picture; even
individual buildings can be oriented in such
a way as to make a meaningful whole and a
proper shelter for a truly collective body.

That brings me back to where I started. For
years I have been distressed by our internal
battles, the planning of Auroville being one
of our specially cherished battlefields! Could
it be that we can at last agree on a 'common
game'? Could we find rules on which we
could agree? Could the grid be a first step in
that direction?

Since the presentation on this concept at the
Residents Assembly in August 2010 I have
been surprised by the warm response of
many. Can we still hope?

Pierre Le Grand, 25th Sept, 2010

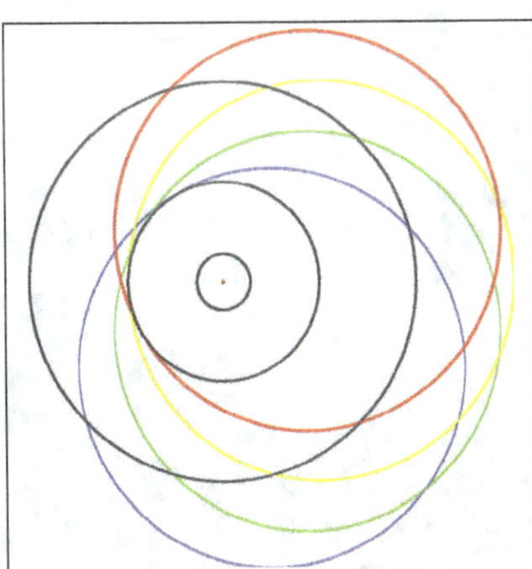

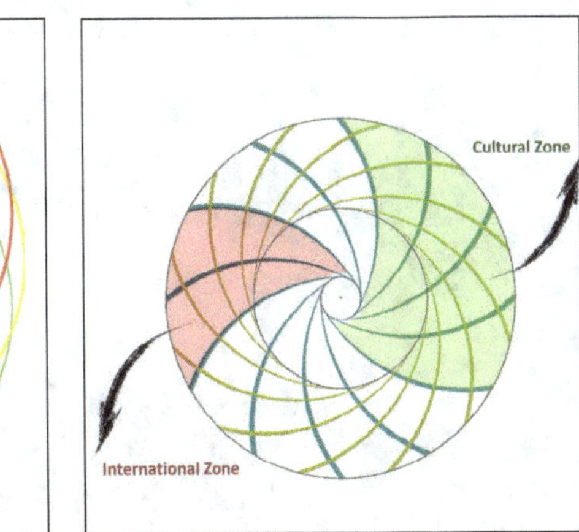

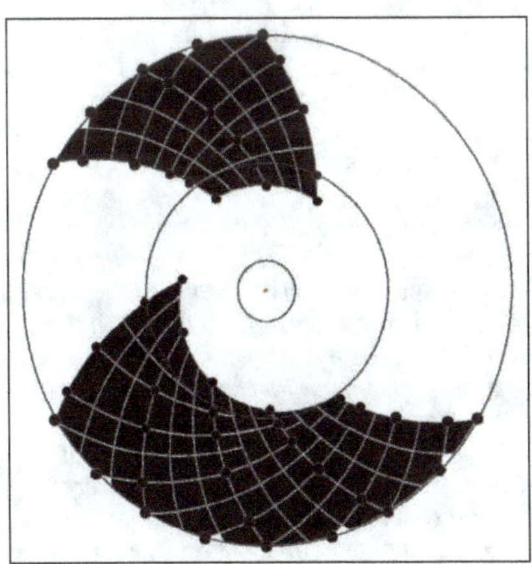

International Zone

"The first aim will therefore be to help individuals to become aware of the fundamental genius of the nation to which they belong and at the same time to bring them into contact with the ways of life of other nations, so that they learn to know and respect equally the true spirit of all the countries of the world."

- The Mother

Unity in diversity

The role of the International Zone is to illustrate in a living, concrete manner, how the principle of unity in diversity is to be applied on the world-scale, at the level of the various nations and cultures which comprise today's humanity.

The role of the pavilions

The pavilions will offer a space for the expression of each nation's search for its soul and its true place in the world. They will be multi-functional, with their foundation in educational programmes, research and cultural activities.

The international section: we have already approached a certain number of ambassadors and countries for each one to have its pavilion - a pavilion from every country. It was an old idea. Some have already accepted, so it is on the way. Each pavilion has its own garden with, as far as possible, a representation of plants and products of the country which it represents. If they have enough money and enough space, they can also have a sort of small museum or permanent exhibition of the

country's achievements. The buildings should be constructed according to the architecture of each country - it should be like a document of information. Then, depending on the money they wish to spend, they could also have accommodation for students, conference rooms, etc., a cuisine of the country, a restaurant of the country - they could have all kinds of developments.

- The Mother

For the 170-acre International Zone, primary development will be limited to national and international cultural pavilions, conference and exhibition halls, communication centres, visitor information centres, parks and green areas, playgrounds, hostels, guest houses, restaurants, kiosks and convenience stores, with the further possibility of medical centres, public transport facilities and some staff quarters.

The adjacent Crown Road area will be used for shopping arcades, restaurants, guest houses, hostels, dwellings and staff quarters, indoor recreation facilities, banking and financial services, parks and green areas. Of the four zones defined by the Galaxy's

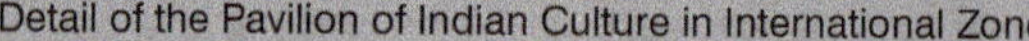

Lines of Force, the International Zone is, so far, the least developed. Understandably, the nature of the other zones - the Industrial Zone with its small scale industries; the Residential Zone with its housing for the residents; and the Cultural Zone with its schools, sports and arts complexes - were of a more basic and urgent priority in the early stages of the township.

The International Zone has been planned on a circular model of four continental areas, with the Pavilion of India, Bharat Nivas, at its centre. Around Bharat Nivas one finds the Americas, Europe (including Russia), Asia with Oceania and Australia, Africa and the Middle East pavilion areas, allowing room for the expression of the fundamental national identity and culture of the various countries of the world.

Contact:
internationalzone@auroville.org.in

Detail of the Pavilion of Indian Culture in International Zone

Education

Auroville wishes to offer itself as a field of ongoing experience and training for the youth of the world, in the inner attitudes and outer methods which are most conducive to the establishment of a culture of peace on earth. In this connection, one of the functions of the International Zone will be to organise and support educational opportunities for and research by visiting students.

Research

Identifying the soul of each nation is at the core of the work of the pavilions. Researchers can take advantage of Auroville as a field of experimentation, discovering in the lively interaction of the International Zone support for "material and spiritual researches for a living embodiment of an actual Human Unity" according to Auroville's Charter.

"Just as each individual has a psychic being which is his true self and which governs his destiny more or less overtly, so too each nation has a psychic being which is its true being and moulds its destiny from behind the veil: it is the soul of the country, the national genius, the spirit of the people, the centre of national aspiration, the fountainhead of all that is beautiful, noble, great and generous in the life of the country."

- The Mother

Map shows a non-finalized International Zone concept, 2010

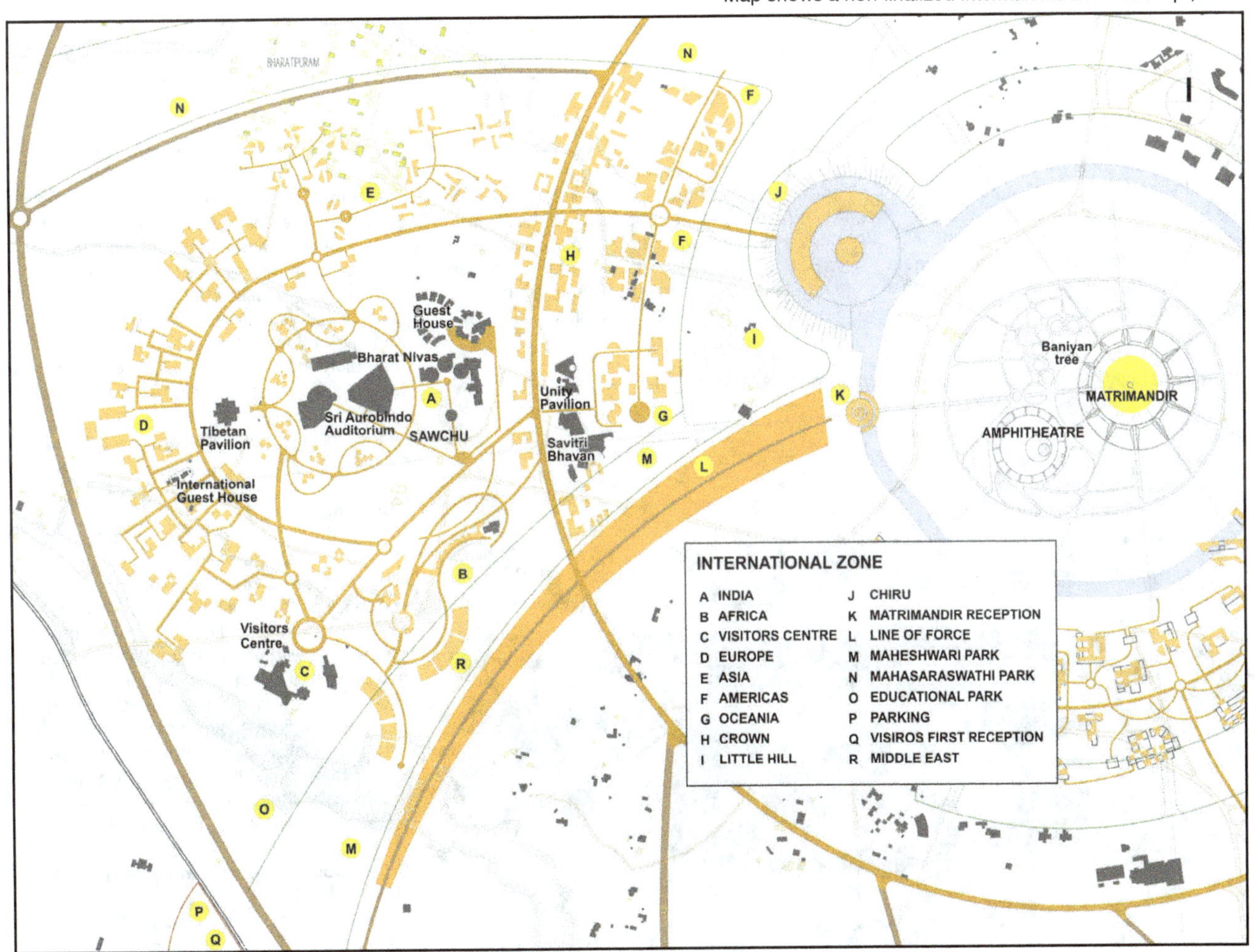

Bharat Nivas, Pavilion of India

Bharat Nivas, the Pavilion of India – planned to embody and symbolically represent the soul of India, both ancient, contemporary and future – was the first construction in the International Zone, the Zone of Union, initiated by the Mother. It started with an auditorium and a restaurant building plus a few other temporary and unfinished structures, and has been fully active since the 1980's. Today the main centres are as follows.

White Hall / Bhavishyaté

The Centre for Research in Indian Culture was the first activity to start in one of the original unfinished buildings, and was then followed by the Centre of Indian Studies. Both Centres functioned together, along with a resource library, to provide space where the international community of Auroville could discover a specifically Indian presence through talks, seminars, exhibitions, workshops, art and cultural projects from different parts of India. Presently these two Centres are temporarily housed in a large open interim space, the White Hall adjacent to the Auditorium, but will soon be shifted to a permanent base now under construction, to be named Bhavishyaté. The White Hall will then become the central area for all-India exhibitions on the themes underlying the International Zone.

Architect: R. Chakrapani

Sri Aurobindo Auditorium under construction

Bhavishyaté will have two floors. The ground floor will house the Centre for Research in Indian Culture, with a small conference room to host workshops, talks and forums covering all aspects of Indian culture, spirituality, creativity and invention; the first floor will house the resource library plus two researchers' rooms, and will meet the needs of the Centre for Indian Studies. Both floors will have open, flexible spaces to hold regular classes, workshops and exhibitions, plus space for study. The building will also include offices and utility spaces plus four rooms for researchers in residence.

Sri Aurobindo Auditorium

The Auditorium is an impressive structure with an iconic roof projection and 650-seat auditorium that provides probably the largest theatre seating capacity in south India. Over the years it has been the scene of creative and innovative programmes plus workshops in music, dance, art and theatre, and has also served as a venue for national and international seminars and as a centre for Indian and international films and film festivals. In fact, it has acted as the cultural heart of Auroville, and the main centre of the International Zone since it started functioning.

Kalakendra

Kalakendra's prime architectural feature is the rounded shape of its main building, that started as a restaurant while also providing space for occasional important meetings. Now it has taken on a new role, as a centre for the arts, with an exhibition space which has proved to be an active hub initiating a wide variety of artistic events, showcasing works in painting, sculpture, pottery and design by Auroville, Indian and international artists. Meanwhile, the plan is to re-activate the space at the top of the building as a restaurant to serve the needs of the campus.

Sri Aurobindo World Centre for Human Unity (SAWCHU)

SAWCHU is a circular shaped unfinished contemporary building that was inaugurated

Completed building in the Bharat Nivas complex, originally envisaged as a restaurant

Entrance to Sri Aurobindo Auditorium

Architect: R. Chakrapani

in 1997 as an offering to India on the occasion of Sri Aurobindo's 125th birth anniversary. Presently it provides space for community interactions and cultural activities, but is planned to become the main exhibition-cum-reception area of the campus on completion.

Tamil Heritage Centre (under construction)
The original plan for Bharat Nivas was to include India's States in the complex in such a way as to highlight the essential unity of the country. This has not been achieved to date, but meanwhile the presence of Tamil Nadu, as Auroville's home state, is seen as essential, and a Centre is under construction. Once completed, it will have exhibition, workshop and conference spaces plus areas for music and dance. It will also have cafeteria and guest facilities.

◀ Bharat Nivas. Clockwise from top left: projecting roof extension, detail of roof extension, White Hall exhibition space, interior working space and east facade.

Indoor entrance area to
Sri Aurobindo Auditorium

Guest facilities
There are two guest houses in the compound, Atithi Griha and Swagatham, to help house artists and others contributing to activities on campus, while also providing accommodation to a regular flow of guests and groups visiting Auroville. Meanwhile, a new temporary guest-cum-cultural facility is coming up in the area where the state buildings were situated in the original plan, aimed at receiving young artists and volunteers in Bharat Nivas, together with people from different States who come to offer workshops and performances in the spaces being provided, and a small open amphitheatre.

The stage in the Sri Aurobindo Auditorium, Bharat Nivas, The Pavilion of India

Kala Kendra, Bharat Nivas, The Pavilion of India, Gallery Square Circle

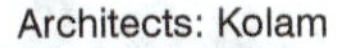
Kala Kendra art exhibition hall

SAWCHU

Originally named as Sri Aurobindo World Centre for Human Unity
(hence acronym) and located in the Bharat Nivas grounds, the
SAWCHU building is today used for a wide variety of Auroville-related
meetings, and also houses some office space.

Architects: Kolam

Centre for Indian Culture

The project, to be completed in 2014, is designed to be a building envelope that will frame the space between the existing Sri Aurobindo Auditorium, the Kalakendra exhibition space and the magnificent boddhi tree that is present near these two buildings, to form a plaza. The long, low volume of the building is a play of voids that will visually link the plaza to the large trees to the north.

The building is elevated from the ground level to enhance the transparency, while the built up volumes are a play of texture and colour between earth, stone and exposed concrete. The natural materials used for all the finishes, including wood from the trees affected by the cyclone of 2012, allows it to blend in with the older buildings.

B.V. Doshi, chairman of the Auroville Town Development Council and member of the Governing Board, was the mentor / critic and general advisor during the conceptual design stage.

The main focal spaces in the building are devoted to

- a seminar space for 40-50 people
- a resource library with the archives of Sri Aurobindo's works

- study and work spaces for resident researchers and teachers
- 2 studio apartments for researchers, and a fraternity house for students

- administrative offices with a 10-12 person meeting room, plus ancillary facilities like pantry

- transition spaces that are open to the gardens for exhibitions / study spaces / small group work and performances.

Architect: Suhasini Ayer-Guigan

Entrance to the Kala Kendra exhibition hall

Entrance road to the Bharat Nivas compound

Atithi Griha

A guest house with 15 rooms in traditional
Indian style, with single, double and family
accommodation, forming part of the Bharat
Nivas campus (see also Guest Houses).

Contact:
Tel: 0413-2622283
e-mail: atithigriha@gmail.com

Atithi Griha Guest House, Architect: Dharmesh Jadeja

International House

The International House in Auroville's International Zone is designed to accommodate longer term volunteers and researchers in an affordable and sustainable way. The complex can house up to 25 people in two dormitory-style buildings with garden, common kitchen, and compost toilets. The first building, which was originally designed to be an element of the Pavilion of the United States, was organized by Auroville International USA through the Design/Build Programme of the University of Washington (Seattle). The University architecture students and faculty designed the building incorporating appropriate technologies and green practices. In January 2002, a team of 42 people from the University came to

Auroville to clear the site and begin the construction in company with Aurovilians and local workers. The University team had to leave after a couple months, and the work continued slowly thereafter for several years, but unexpectedly a redesign of the International Zone then placed the United States Pavilion in another location. As a solution, the International House was conceived as a project of the US Pavilion Group. A second building was constructed in 2010 so the complex could function as a self-supporting service for the International Zone and Auroville. The new building plugged directly into the existing rainwater harvesting and solar electrical and hot water systems, and added more showers and compost

toilets. This new dormitory added another dimension to the eco-design by using "waste" materials in the construction. The ground plus three-floor A frame construction is entirely roofed by corrugated sheets made from used tetrapak containers recycled into roofing. Local wood, and "waste" materials like used styrofoam (polystyrene), and even discarded petrol hoses, have been used in the construction. Both buildings have unique qualities that are very different, and yet are complimentary in relation to their purpose and eco-friendly zero waste orientation.

Contact:
internationalzone@auroville.org.in

Roofing of International House

Complete roofing span of International House

International House, with water tower

Architects: Architecture Department, University of Washington, USA

Pavilion of Tibetan Culture

Located in the International Zone behind the Bharat Nivas complex, the Pavilion of Tibetan Culture is presently the most completely functional of the Cultural / National Pavilions.

In December 1993, His Holiness the Dalai Lama, Patron of the Pavilion, came to Auroville to lay the foundation stone, and personally made a substantial financial contribution at the time towards its manifestation. Construction started in June 1997.

Today regular cultural activities are held in the Pavilion to open a window on the ancient culture of Tibet, and to reflect the aspirations and achievements of the Tibetan people and their cultural contributions to the world. Also, many Tibetan students have been trained there in different skills - like appropriate building technology, afforestation and environmental protection, etc.
Already in 1973, while visiting the Sri Aurobindo Ashram in Pondicherry, the Dalai Lama said:

"We are deeply impressed by the spiritual aim behind the building of an international city called Auroville. The importance of the effort to achieve human unity and international co-operation by the creation of such a city cannot be over-emphasised; nor can we neglect the benefit to be acquired from it. We are therefore very keen to be the first country to build a pavilion.
We understand that this pavilion will be dedicated to the essence of Tibetan culture in an effort to show that out of the diversity of world cultures, these pavilions can help to create a new harmony towards world human unity."

- H.H. The Dalai Lama, 1973

Contact:
Tel: 0413-2622401, 2623338
kalsang@auroville.org.in

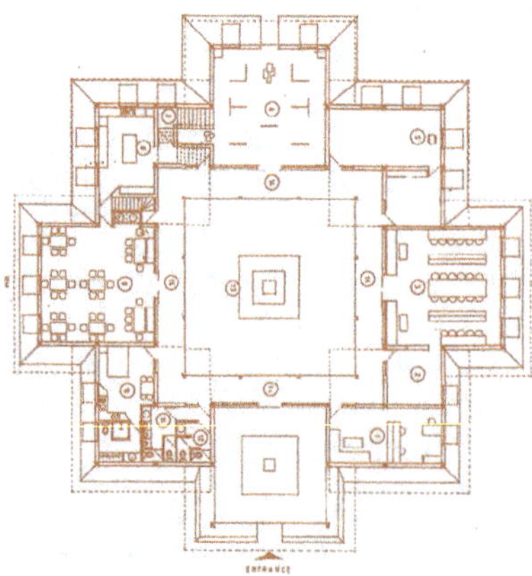

H.H. The Dalai Lama laying the foundation stone

Architects: André Hababou and Satprem Maini

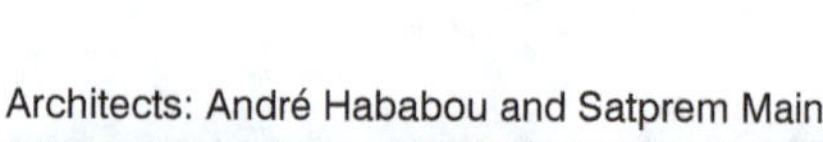

The Unity Pavilion

The 'Unity Pavilion', located on the Crown Road in the International Zone, was started as a seed and catalyst for the overall development of Auroville's International Zone. Today it consists of the Unity Hall, the Hall of Peace, office space, a Geodesic Dome, an outdoor eating space, and hosts a wide variety of events.

The Unity Hall offers space for a wide range of activities such as exhibitions, cultural events, presentations and lectures, workshops and community meetings. The Hall can hold up to 250 people and has proved to be very versatile in its use.

The Hall of Peace was inaugurated on 11 February 2014 and is the home for the Peace Table of Asia. Regular "Peace" meditations take place, and other programmes around the Peace Table are being developed.

The office building provides office space for the Unity Pavilion management team, Peace Research, the International Zone Coordination Team, Pavilion Groups, Auroville International, SAVI (Auroville's reception for Volunteers and Interns), and Koodam (Auroville's platform for conflict resolution and facilitation).

The Geodesic Dome is used for outdoor circle meetings and dialogue sessions, and the

outdoor eating space for evening gatherings and cultural events that include food and refreshments.

The focus of the work in the Unity Pavilion covers topics such as human unity, world peace, east-west and north-south relations, sustainable development and human potential, development of the International Zone, and the interaction of cultures that defy national borders.

"It is no longer towards division and difference that we should turn our minds, but on unity, union, even oneness necessary for the pursuit and realisation of a common ideal..."
(Sri Aurobindo, A Message to America, 1949)

Architects: Piero & Gloria Cicionesi

Hall of Peace

In the early 1980s, the American master woodworker George Nakashima had bought two huge logs of 300-year old Eastern Black Walnut, and was inspired by their richly grained quality to use them in their full length and width as Altars of Peace, each measuring approximately 3.3 by 3.3 metres to fully express the texture, natural shape and free edges of the wood. Following a dream involving Sri Aurobindo, he planned that the Altars would be placed one on each continent, providing places for people from all religions and faiths to gather together in prayer or silent meditation for peace around the world.

The project took off in 1984, and the first Altar of Peace, the Altar for North America, was placed in the Cathedral of St. John the Divine in New York and dedicated on New Year's Eve, 1986, in an impressive ceremony with a Concert for Peace in the presence of diplomats from many countries and representatives of many faiths.

After George Nakashima's passing his daughter and son continued his legacy, and after much delay the second table, the Table for Europe, was finally installed in June 1991 in the Russian Academy of Arts in Moscow, and the search then began for where to place the third table, the Table for Asia.

In the late 1990s, when work had already started on this third Peace Table, the Table for Asia, some Aurovilians discussed with the Nakashima Foundation the possibility of Auroville hosting it, on the grounds that George Nakashima had been a disciple of Sri Aurobindo and The Mother and Auroville seemed an ideal location. The Nakashima Foundation responded positively, and agreed to donate both the Table and the transportation costs. This resulted in the Table being inaugurated in Auroville on 29th February 1996 - the day which the Mother has called 'The Golden Day', when in 1956 the manifestation of the Supramental occurred upon earth. However, it was not until February 2014 that the table finally came to rest as the centre piece in the completed Hall of Peace, designed by Piero and Gloria Cicionesi, a circular building attached to the Unity Pavilion which was inaugurated on 11th February 2014.

Contact: 0413-2623576, unity@auroville.org.in

Architect: Helmut Schmid

Savitri Bhavan

Situated in the International Zone between Bharat Nivas and Matrimandir, Savitri Bhavan is a centre of education based on the vision and teachings of Sri Aurobindo and the Mother. Its purpose is to gather all kinds of materials and activities that will foster knowledge and understanding of the lives, work and vision of Sri Aurobindo and the Mother and the aims and ideals of Auroville, and make them available to the interested general public.

The Savitri Bhavan campus is located on the Crown, south of the Unity Pavilion. Its facilities have been developed on the basis of a Master Plan created in 1996. A small multipurpose building inaugurated in August 1999 currently houses a Reading Room and Digital Library. A large hall was opened in November 2004 and later integrated into the main building, which was inaugurated in 2008. The main building also contains a picture gallery dedicated to exhibiting the Meditations on Savitri paintings (prepared under the guidance of the Mother from 1961 to 1970 and entrusted to the Bhavan by the artist, Huta, in 2001), and an amphitheatre for gatherings and performances, as well as classrooms and offices for staff and researchers, but remains to be completed by the construction of an auditorium with multimedia facilities, to be known as the 'Sangam Hall'. A hostel to accommodate visiting researchers and students was inaugurated in 2012.

For more photos and information on the architecture, history and activities, see www.savitribhavan.org.

Contact:
Savitri Bhavan, Auroville 605101,
Tamil Nadu, India
Tel: +91 0413 2622922
Email: savitribhavan@auroville.org.in

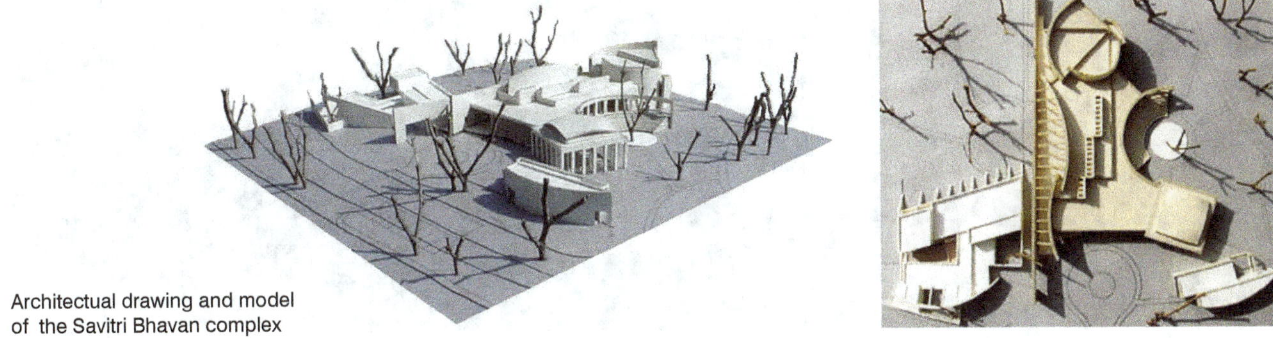

Architectual drawing and model
of the Savitri Bhavan complex

Amphitheatre

Clockwise: Amphitheatre and facade, Library, Exhibition Hall, Entrance with Sri Aurobindo statue, Reception

Savitri Bhavan Hostel

Hostel facilities include 7 single rooms,
2 double rooms, 1 room for resident
caretaker - all with bathrooms,
kitchen/dining facilities and utilities.

Industrial Zone

The 363-acre Industrial Zone, located in the north-east of the township, though the smallest of the four zones of Auroville, has the maximum amount of land features. It has the most canyons, has low-lying waterlogged lands, and has excellent farm land. The rich soil in its environs has given rise to the neighbouring villages of Bharatipuram and Alankuppam.

Upasana Design Studio

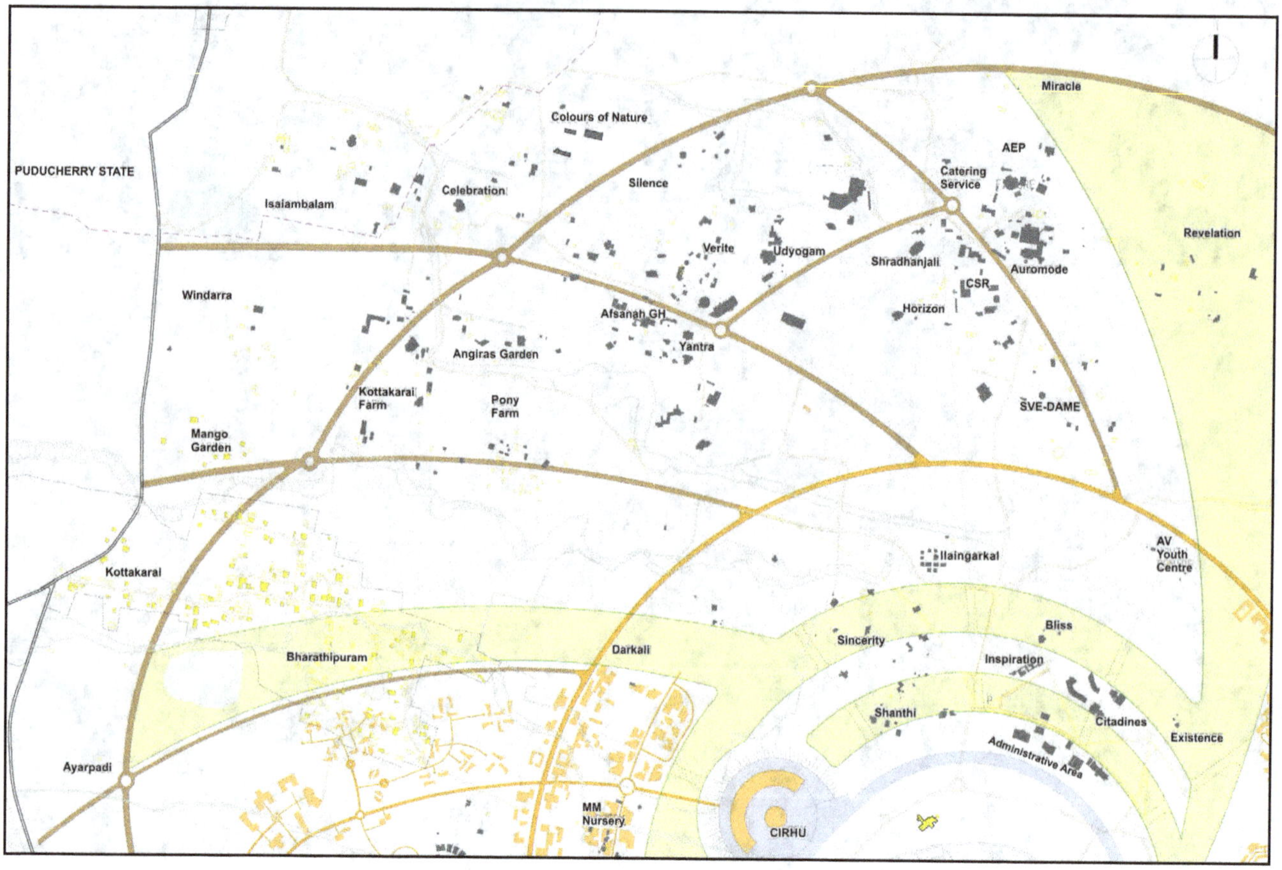

The location of the Industrial Zone in this area has therefore been a challenge to Auroville, which aims at turning it into a win-win situation for all, thereby making it a model for other "industrial zones" elsewhere to follow. Instead of an "industrial zone" with the rather negative connotations of dirt, pollution, ugly concrete, factory-like buildings and a deserted feeling in the evenings, we are now speaking of the Auroshilpam Economic Zone as one which will be ecologically sensitive, lively and beautiful. It is essentially a low-level, non-polluting, manufacturing zone where offices will be located for research and development, where samples and prototypes will be developed, and where management will be housed. The bulk of the manufacturing will be outsourced to areas where labour is more immediately available. The Zone should ideally provide employment to Aurovilians who are producing goods to cater to the needs of the growing township. In addition to production units, there will also be substantial social infrastructure, like crèches, canteens, kiosks and convenience stores, internet facilities, guest houses, staff quarters, and sports and recreational facilities for those living and working in the area. It should all result in a zone with a different, harmonious vibration of energy conducive to working and living.

At present about 35 units employing some 600 local people are located in the Zone. All the units are part of the Auroville Foundation, and are expected to contribute a third of their profits to Auroville. Their activities include producing and marketing garments, leather goods, furniture, pottery items, food & health products, solar photovoltaic systems, prefabricated ferrocement elements, earth-technology components for building, computer peripherals & software, architectural services, renewable energy products, incense, stationery, etc. There are also two other recognised Economic Zones located near Kuilapalayam Village and Koot Road, which house another 50 units also functioning under the umbrella of the Auroville Foundation. Since a few years now the Industrial Zone has had an Industrial Zone Group (IZG) consisting of 4-5 committed Aurovilians looking into all

Auromode

Architect: André Hababou

the aspects of the area, to ensure growth that is finely balanced between the vision of the Galaxy Master Plan and ground realities. Apart from framing guidelines for harmonious long-term growth with the surrounding villages, it also deals with the day-to-day problems and requests of people who want to set up units in the Zone. Where can the unit be best located? What is its impact on the environment? Where does it get its water from? What are its electricity demands? What kind of traffic is to be

expected? Will there be sound pollution, and how can it be mitigated? Does the unit intend to build caretaker houses or staff quarters to avoid dead zones after working hours? Are the finances sufficient to pay for the buildings and the extensive infrastructure?
These are the challenges, and they all have to be taken into account if the Zone is to become an area of positive contribution to Auroville.

Contact: izg@auroville.org.in

Centre for Scientific Research (Completed 1986)

Avatar Syrups entry

Cultural Zone

The 250-acre Cultural Zone will have its own specific vibration, emanating from the various cultural institutions and research centres related to education, the arts and sport that are planned there. City level cultural facilities will find their place there, such as auditoriums and exhibition halls, parks and playgrounds, green areas, kiosks and convenience stores, a stadium and large spaces with sports facilities.

Concept

Although the search for a higher and truer way of living and culture is a dominant theme for the entire Auroville township, the artistic and educational aspects of this research are to be pursued with a greater focus in the Cultural Zone, which is meant to explore the fruits of all cultures through their diverse expressions in music, dance, painting, sculpture, theatre, etc, and develop new cultural expressions, combining the areas of the arts, education and sports.

Cultural Zone today

At present, the educational facilities in the Cultural Zone comprise a pre-creche, 2 creches, 3 kindergartens, 2 primary plus elementary schools, and a full-fledged sports complex. In addition, there is a secondary school campus that houses Future School and Last School, the latter since the summer of 2014.

A Youth Centre, a Music Studio, and a Centre for Performing Arts have also been created in the Cultural Zone. Additionally, 'Kalabhumi', an artists' settlement, has been constructed to provide studios and space for different art forms, with staff quarters and a gallery. At present, Kalabhumi offers studios for sculpture, metal work, painting, drawing, music practice and an amphitheatre with seating arrangements for around 150 people.

Kalabhumi: Top Aurofilm and Music Studio below.

Kalabhumi: Aurofilm and Painting Studio

Tomorrow
In the future, the Cultural Zone will house additional primary and secondary education facilities for an estimated 5,400 children, as well as a university, science laboratories, academies for music, dance and theatre, artistic centres for fine arts, martial arts, an institute for photographic, video and film production, specialised libraries, and a sports stadium.

Cultural boulevard
The Crown Road section of this zone is envisioned as a pedestrian 'cultural boulevard', to be lined with exhibition halls, art galleries, theatres, libraries, archives, guest houses, green spaces, offices for SAIIER, and staff quarters.

Land situation in the Cultural Zone
As in all Zones of the Auroville Township, presently not all the land in the Cultural Zone belongs to Auroville. So far, Auroville has been able to secure 200 acres, and another 40 acres has yet to be purchased.

Architect: David Nightingale

CRIPA - Centre for Research in the Performing Arts

CRIPA is a project of SAIIER located in Kalabhumi, with a rehearsal hall, educational facility and research centre devoted to music, dance and theatre. It is the first building of a larger planned Performing Arts Centre.

Contact: e-mail jillswar@auroville.org.in

Residential Zone

For the 412-acre Residential Zone, development will be primarily limited to residential community buildings, community meeting spaces, crèches and young age group educational needs, work studios, first aid centres, parks, playgrounds, landscaping elements, eco-friendly parking areas, kiosks and convenience stores, with the additional possibility of small handicraft ateliers.

The adjacent Crown Road area is planned for dwellings and city level retail stores, display areas, communication and recreation centres, restaurants, libraries and reading rooms, health centres, essential utility needs, city management sub-offices for services such as fire, water, sanitation and post/telecom, parks and green areas and eco-friendly parking. There could also be guest houses, department stores, some small professional offices, utility maintenance centres and essential transport-related infrastructure and conference facilities.

House in Samasti

Housing in Prarthna, Sukhavati and ▶
Invocation settlement

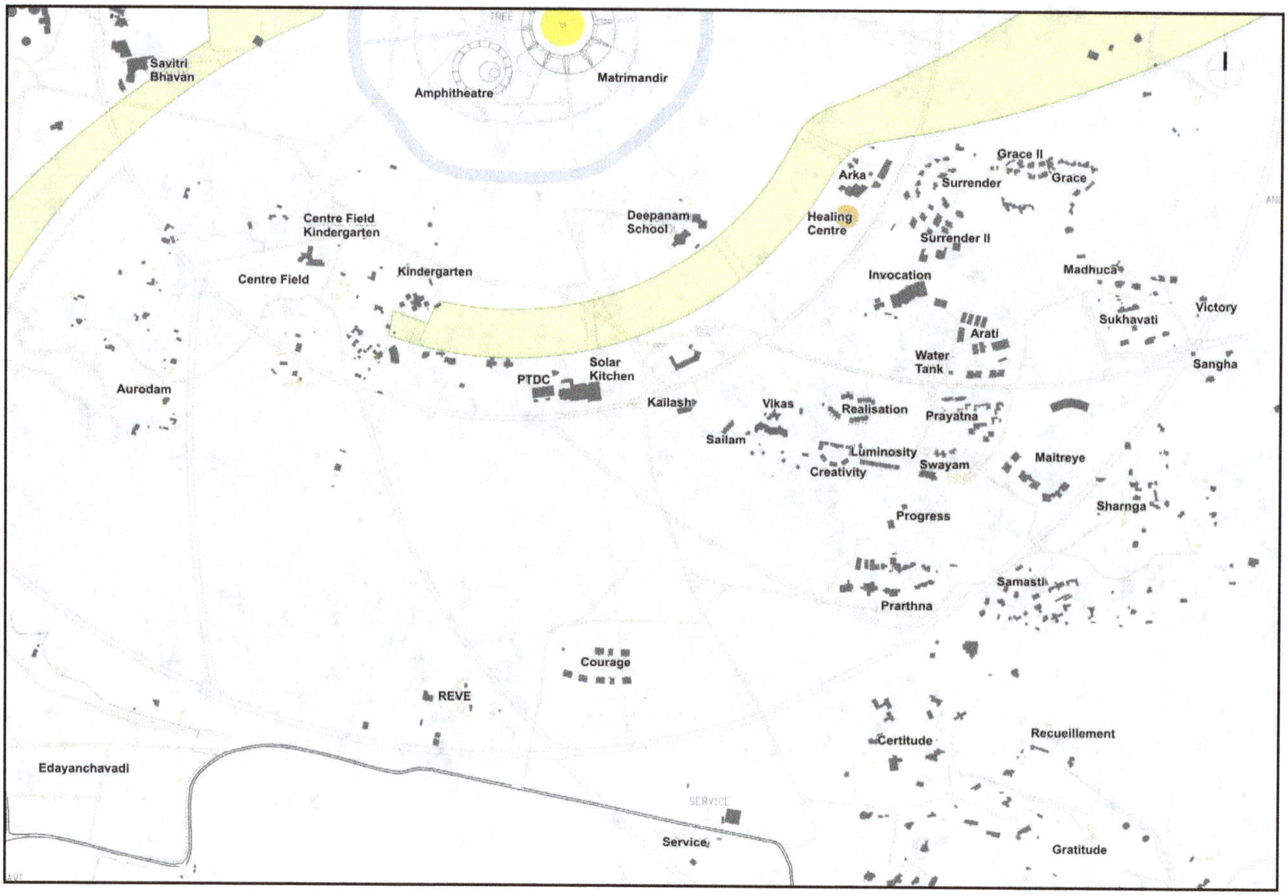

Samasti was collectively envisaged by a group of architects, town planners and people keen to live together and be part of an experiment that could change the trend of habitation, with benefits to the future township. Much time and many discussions later, three architects – Suhasini, Ajit and Peter – designed parts of the project separately, exchanging ideas on those decisions that would influence the neighbourhood as a whole.

Houses in Samasti and Grace settlement

Grace settlement

Vikas settlement apartments

Surrender settlement

Creativity

Settlement apartments

Creativity is a low cost community housing complex which was completed in 2004. It is composed of 12 single units, 8 couple units, 1 family unit, a unit for 5 persons sharing facilities and 5 guest rooms. It also includes a community kitchen, shared laundry, a multi purpose hall, an art studio, a therapy room/library and office and storage space.

Architect: Anupama Kundoo

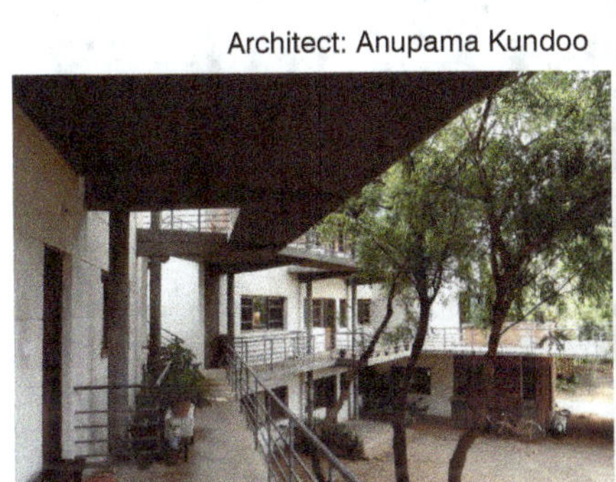

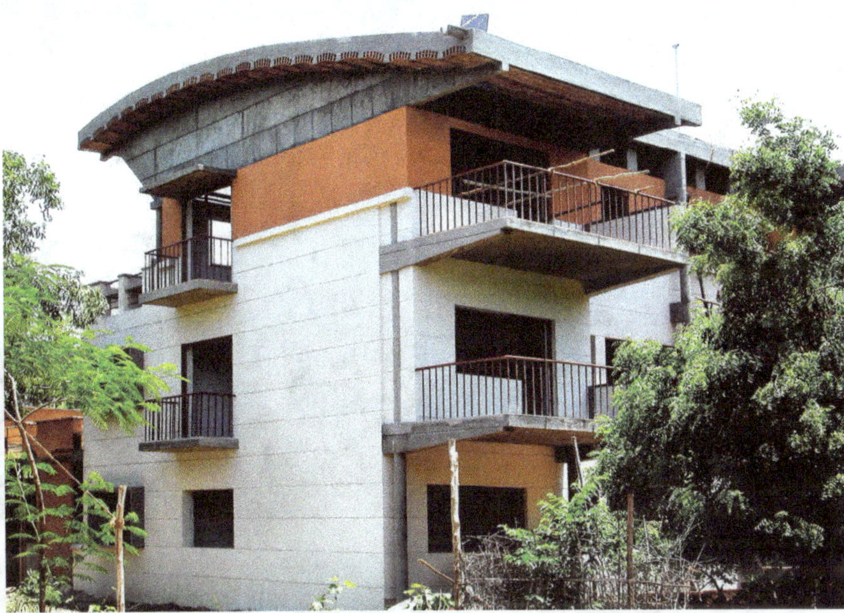

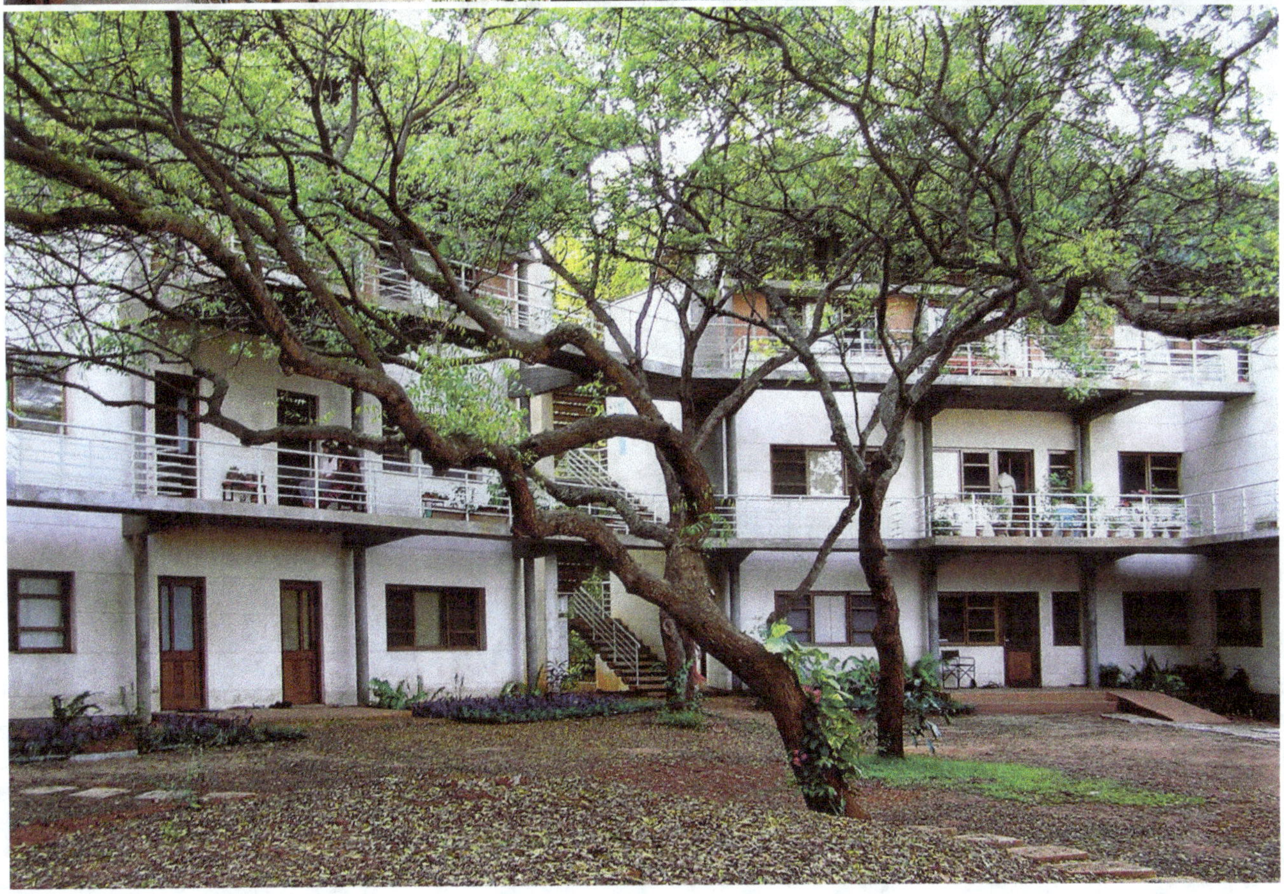

Citadines

The concept of Citadines is an alternative way of approaching residence and community building. While being rational, practical and easy to maintain, the project rests on the foundation of maintaining the basic ideals of Auroville. The prime criterion to live in Citadines is to be dedicated to Auroville.

In exchange for this dedication, fully furnished flats, decorated with beauty-in-simplicity, and provided with collective services such as covered parking, laundry service, reception desk, multi-purpose hall, complete maintenance of flats, buildings and gardens, etc, have been provided. The basic concept is that the time, energy and resources of residents who are fully dedicated to the growth of Auroville is not scattered or inefficiently used.

The first phase of Citadines, planned to house 50-60 people, comprises two apartment buildings, each consisting of a ground floor plus three storeys, with a total residential built-up area of approx 2,000 sq.m, with approx 1,300 sq.m. area for various community facilities on the ground floor of each block. The design incorporates various solar passive techniques and building materials to have low mechanical energy usage and climatically comfortable interiors. There are three types of apartment:

- 12 nos. singles' apartments each with usable area of approx 30 sq.m.
- 6 nos. 2-bed apartments, each of approx 60 sq.m.
- 6 nos. 2-bed apartments, each of approx 90 sq.m.

All the apartments have 7-10 sq.m. of covered balcony area and also 14 sq.m. of terrace gardens in addition to the usable area.

The entire project has been financed by donations, to allow Auroville to further its collective research towards a fraternal economy.

On a practical level:
- Money was not the criterion for allocating residences.
- The "client/builder" relationship was eliminated.
- Auroville takes care of its committed citizens.
- Residents are freed from "domestic" chores, and so have more time and energy to give to Auroville's needs.
- There is no sense of personal ownership, but rather a sense of sharing a collective asset of Auroville.

- The sense of mobility is enhanced as it is easy to change from one flat to another or from one building to another as time goes by, and the situation of the occupants changes.
- The flats were offered with no exchange of money.
- General maintenance is handled through a central 'Citadines Fund'.

Choosing the residents of Citadines was a delicate task, to which the project holders in consultation with the Housing Service gave their full attention. Aurovilians, Newcomers and Long Term Guests were eligible. Dedication to Auroville and to meeting the needs of the candidate were the prime criteria. Attention was also paid to keeping a balance between the above mentioned categories of residents.

Contact: louis@auroville.org.in
aryamani@auroville.org.in

Luminosity

A special place for living and working

Luminosity is located in the Residential Zone of Auroville, and consists of 11 offices on the ground floor, 6 apartments on each of the first and second floors, and a partially-covered communal roof.

The aim of the project was to provide simple, rich and beautiful spaces for the residents to live and work in, whilst trying to balance the often contradictory needs of community and privacy. With this in mind, the offices have been located on the ground floor to negate the need for individual gardens and fences, thus allowing anyone to walk around the building as they choose, whilst nurturing Auroville's ideal of 'Not belonging to anyone in particular, but to humanity as a whole'. The staircases are spatially more generous than usual - as an invitation to the residents to use the communal roof, which has been conceived as an extension of the living-room space. This roof is divided into a 'quiet' half and a 'social' half, and has a laundry area and a garden at each end, as well as covered areas for relaxing and socialising.

Aside from a number of measures taken to reduce acoustic transmission between the apartments, the building aims to be independent from the water mains. This has been achieved through the re-use of grey-water for watering plants and flushing toilets, as well as by utilising a 350,000 litre rainwater catchment tank to supply each resident with 100 litres of water per day throughout the year.

Architects: David Nightingale & Ganesh Bala

Swayam

Swayam was started early in 2003 with the aim of creating a small mixed-use residential community for a diverse group of Aurovilians happy to live and work in a humble environment that is sustainable & ecologically sound. Final go-ahead was received in 2009.

From the outset, the plan was to build with certain principles and materials, and to demonstrate that a low-rise high-density development on a small scale suits Auroville well at this stage.

The project consists of varying types of houses that include ground floor working studios and living areas with sleeping space above, plus small flats for singles, couples or a small family. Complementing the living space is community infrastructure such as a meeting pavilion designed in the Japanese style, a rock garden, and some art installations in public spaces, donated by visiting and Auroville artists. There are also motifs on earth walls, waste water treatment with landscaping of all common areas, and spaces around existing trees, with the layout of houses adjusted to enjoy and not damage any existing planted areas, making the whole project very special for everyone who has been involved or is now living there. Not surprisingly, it has attracted an excellent mix of residents, including Aurovilians, Newcomers and volunteers, with design studios and/or work spaces for individuals in the houses according to individual needs.

Materials used in construction and finishing reflect a quest for beauty with simplicity that has a feel of abundance & generosity. Incorporated in the project have been stabilized earth blocks, terracotta tube vaults, brick vaults, terracotta hollow block jack arches, simple oxide floors, natural stone, and jalis designed from waste materials.

Swayam is one of those rare projects where the design philosophy has been based on belief in clients as the main decision makers, with the architects and builders simply facilitating the process of creating the sort of humble but practical and pleasant-to-live-and-work-in dwellings that people dream of in Auroville.

Architect: Dharmesh Jadeja

A Fine Blending Of Opposites:

As Indian architecture emerges through its challenges of identity & contemporary relevance, we see our practice at Dustudio (formerly Buildaur) in Auroville as ever evolving in the international context of Community life while respecting & learning from traditions that keep you rooted in your context. Dustudio is a collaborative practice that takes its inspiration from ancient Indian wisdom & art of building where form is the creation of the spirit and draws all its meaning and value from the infinite spirit. An attempt to achieve a synthesis between traditional ways of designing and building while responding to the contemporary context that is climatically appropriate,

Dustudio, Swayam

energy efficient & creates a conscious space for artisans to participate in this process of creation.

Our practice strives to work joyfully together with a team of professionals, dedicated to the ideal of unending education by various ways of learning, acquiring and sharing knowledge through research, interactions & enquiry. We consciously work with like-minded organisations to create aesthetic, holistic living environment through a rigorous participatory design process with our clients and collaborators, learning from each other's expertise and widening the base of our knowledge.

Architect: Dharmesh Jadeja

Realization

The Realization housing project began with the aim of providing economical housing in the form of 70 apartments for around 170 people, mostly young Aurovilians and Newcomers. Totally 16 apartments are being developed in the first phase:
6 single room from 38 to 43 sq.m.
3 two-room from 52 to 57.7 sq.m.
7 three-room from 70 to 84.3 sq.m.
Ground floor apartments with garden, and first floor apartments with a terrace, plu pergola, have been completed, all using compressed stabilized earth blocks (CSEBs). Costing came out at Rs.17,000 per sq.m carpet area, including basic finishing and infrastructure and Auroville contributions.
What made this project unique at the outset was the invitation to future inhabitants to actually participate directly in the construction of their own apartments, thereby helping to keep costs down while also giving a more "personal" commitment to the construction process. More than 200 people from 25 countries became involved, mostly in making the needed CSEBs.
The project, completed in 2012, includes shared facilities in the form of a communal building of 2-3 rooms, laundry, storeroom, covered parking shed, rainwater harvesting, solid waste facility, and an innovative earth tunnel under the rainwater holding tank, via which cooling air can be drawn into the building to reduce interior temperatures by up to 10°C.

Architect:
Satprem Maïni

Arati III

Encouraging interaction

Forming part of a larger community of apartment buildings, Arati III is the 'outer face' of the community. Carrying the role of an interactive building on the streetscape, the design goal has been to enable street-side interaction with the residents. All living room balconies face the street while the quieter areas such as the bedrooms and study face inner gardens. Passers-by can chat to friends on the balconies. An open central staircase opens the building to both the inner gardens as well as the outer street. One of the key features of this project is the multiple levels at which the apartments are set, creating for each apartment an individual landing foyer without having a neighbour directly opposite. The other key features are its box balconies which allow just enough space to open the long French windows and sit out. The boxing of the balconies also gives additional protection against the harsh sun and monsoon rains, preventing either from entering the rooms.

Integrating other infrastructural features such as storm water management, waste water recycling and re-use, and a low maintenance garden, Arati 3 encourages interaction between people without compromising on privacy or noise intrusion.

Total built up area: 1,740 sqm
Total number of apartments: 12

Architect: Shama Dalvi

"/>

Maitreye

Maitreye is a residential project situated in Auroville's Residential Zone, aimed at providing various types of housing for approx 250 people in phase 1, with units for single persons, couples and families. It aims to "cater for the needs of Newcomers and Aurovilians with limited financial resources" by use of cost-effective construction methods. This includes use of random rubble masonry rather than reinforced concrete foundations, and making the whole structure load-bearing (frame construction has only been used for lateral ties against earthquake forces). External walls are constructed by laying two hollow fired bricks side by side, creating two different cavities to dampen sound and provide thermal insulation. To avoid high humidity, all the houses have cross-ventilation. Also, the rooms have high ceilings with windows opening at different heights to maximize air flow. The roof slabs are made of hollow terracotta blocks for insulation, and to minimise the need for costly concrete. The project's infrastructure includes a water treatment system and a rainwater harvesting tank, the latter feeding a common laundry.

Architect: Sonali Phadnis

Maitreye II

Maitreye 2 Phase 1 is a housing project for Newcomers in Auroville, providing 27 apartments on three floors with common facilities, parking, and a mini park at the back of the building that can serve also the surrounding communities. The project has been planned to include apartments for singles (about 60 sq.m), couples (about 90 sq.m) and families (about 120 sq.m). In total it will be able to provide accommodation for some 50 residents, occupying altogether 2,100 sq.m.

The architectural concept behind the design has been to have maximum ventilation, combined with very well planned and organized space inside the apartments.

Styling of the building incorporates traditional elements like louvres on the front façade to cut down penetrating sunlight, similar to many of the colonial buildings seen in this part of India.

This is Phase 1 of a larger project, which will extend to the outer Ring Road, with beautiful gardens between the building itself and the Vikas radial.

Overall, the building has been planned not only for its pleasing architecture, but to be very cost-effective.

Construction time 2013 - 2014

Architect: Pino Marchese

Inspiration

Inspiration is a collective housing project under construction in the residential area of Auroville. When finished, it will have 15 apartments of approx. 50 sq.m. each with 250 sq.m. common space, which includes laundry, multipurpose hall with common television and dining facilities on the ground floor.

Three apartments on the ground floor are accessed by a ramp.

A lot of attention is paid in ensuring that outside walls are shaded wherever possible; a rooftop pergola will shade the southern and western sides of the building.

Also the building is designed as four different blocks accessed by one staircase and connecting passageways. The scattered form gives the needed privacy to the apartments with no shared walls, and a single staircase gives the feeling of one family, to reinforce the spirit of collective living in Auroville. All apartments face onto green spaces on both sides. The long and narrow-built form takes advantage of the prevailing winds to ensure cross ventilation in all the rooms. The project will also have a waste water treatment system.

Architect: Sonali Phadnis

Prayatna II

Werner Stoff, architect of Prayatna II, is convinced that only in a suitable living space can self development of a human be possible. Only in the right environment can the healing and harmonizing effect of beauty grow. His space ideal is when the room is an extension of the self, and he sees this also as a protection against the outside world. Most rooms today have only a functional aspect; everything is planned and designed to obey only this single rule, leaving no space for the soul.

Werner designs more from an inner level, and is convinced that architecture has a role to play in helping people enjoy a more fulfilled life. His abstract sculptures are not just formal expressions, but are shaped by a more inner vision that makes them expressions of an inner world. They seek to give us insight into more subtle and inner movements that are not visible to our eyes. Werner Stoff, who has a Freemason background, worked as an architect and designer in Cologne in Germany before coming to live in Auroville in 2004, where he has created a design and architectural unit to work on several township projects.

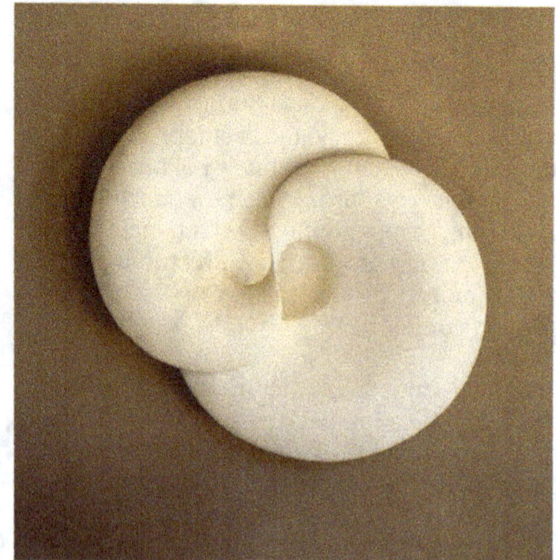

Architect: Werner Stoff

Public buildings

Visitors Centre

The Auroville Visitors Centre, which was constructed in 1991 with grants and other help from HUDCO, Ministry for Non-Conventional Energy Sources, Indian Navy, United Nations Centre for Human Settlement, Commission of the European Union (via BORDA), German Appropriate Technology Exchange, Stichting De Zaair, and Foundation for World Education, is Auroville's reception and information-disseminating centre for the hundreds - often thousands - of tourists and visitors coming to Auroville daily. It is a popular and pleasant complex specifically designed for visitors from all over the world, with the local climate, materials and building skills influencing the design. Special emphasis has been placed on natural lighting and ventilation in the building, as renewable energy sources were to be used.

From the outset, the plan for the building was to limit the use of concrete and steel, but this was easier said than done, for in a compression structure the construction of arches, vaults and domes

Seating for open air theatre

is necessitated. Prefabricated ferrocement elements were used for all doors and overhangs, thereby doing away with the use of wood. A 4-metre grid using load-bearing pillars and arched or corbelled openings was made with stabilised compressed earth blocks to reduce costs. Solar, wind and biomass energy, water management

Architects: Suhasini Ayer-Guigan & Satprem Maïni

and recycling techniques, mud and ferrocement technology, and reclamation and afforestation were all integrated in the process. Stabilised earth blocks for domes and prefabricated ferrocement channels were considered as the best solution for roofing. It was felt the resulting sequence of arcaded and semi-covered spaces would give a clear sense of direction to people, while at the same time demonstrating and promoting the rich potential of alternative technologies in its construction, with particular emphasis on the use of mud as a building material.

Today the main building comprises a popular multi-cuisine cafeteria at ground level, a night time community space cum economical eatery upstairs, 3 boutiques displaying and selling Auroville handicrafts, a bookshop, a guest accommodation service and Matrimandir booking facility with admin office for the complex, a permanent exhibition on Sri Aurobindo and the Mother, and outdoor exhibitions on Auroville's International Zone and environmental issues.

Following construction of the main building, in 2004 an exhibition hall was added, with information desk, exhibition spaces, video auditorium, and more recently an extension devoted to Matrimandir information and video showing, as well as an exhibition highlighting some of Auroville's best practices. The compound also hosts an organic coffee bar, a tea shop and a cycle rental facility.

View across open-air theatre space

Contact:
Tel: 0413-2622239
avinfoservice@auroville.org.in

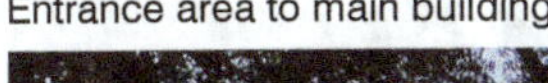
Entrance area to main building

Visitors Centre restaurant

Entrance to the Information Centre

Interior Exhibition Hall of the ►
Information Centre

◄ Boutique d'Auroville
Dreamer's Café and
Information Centre building

Model of the Matrimandir and
Matrimandir Garden

Town Hall

While during Auroville's first forty-plus years the residents performed their various administrative tasks in a wide variety of make-shift places throughout the area, the township presently prides itself on having a large, spacey and efficacious set-up, known as the Town Hall complex, in Auroville's administrative area in the centre of the city, just north of the Matrimandir. A larger Town Hall is foreseen at a much later stage, of which this first phase will be the forerunner.

The present Town Hall complex, looking out on the Matrimandir and its gradually emerging gardens, consists of two robust, separate, but interconnected structures: the **Centre for Urban Research**, completed in 2002, and the **Multimedia Centre**, which reached completion in 2004. In between the two, facilities for a cafeteria have been created.

Town Hall with Multimedia Centre beyond

Centre for Urban Research, alias Town Hall
The Auroville Centre for Urban Research
(Annex to the future Town Hall and hence
commonly referred to as Town Hall)
came into being through funding by the
European Commission, as part of the 'Asia
Urbs Programme', in which Auroville's
town planning unit Auroville's Future (now
named L'avenir d'Auroville) took part at the
beginning of the century.

The original design expanded through
support from Holland-based NGO Stichting
de Zaaier and various Auroville resources,
which enabled other than town planning
facilities to be sited in the building.

The building has a covered surface of 1,300
sqm plus 350 sqm of verandas, and consists
of 3 floors. It presently houses: L'avenir
d'Auroville, Auroville's Financial Service,
Auroville Fund, Land Services, Project
Coordination Group, offices of the Working
Committee and Auroville Council, FAMC,
Housing Service, Auroville Security, and
Auroville Radio, with various meeting rooms.

Multimedia Centre

Construction of the Multimedia Centre
(MMC) adjacent to the Town Hall was
enabled through a large donation from
Gateway Group around the turn of the
millennium, specified for activities pertaining
to communication. Since its completion,
various services have left their temporary
work spaces elsewhere in the township

Architects: Anupama Kundoo

Bronze sculpture by Robert Lorrain

and moved into their new abodes, which
find themselves spread out over two
floors with a surface of 224 and 227 sqm
plus verandas. These are: studios of the
Auroville website and intranet (Auronet),
editors of Auroville's weekly News & Notes
bulletin, OutreachMedia press office, Auro-
Traductions' translating services, video
library, music library, as well as offices of
the Entry Service, Residents Service and
Avdzines graphics unit and photocopying
facility.

Last but not least, the MMC includes a 154
sqm multi-purpose auditorium-cum-viewing
theatre with large screen and seating for up
to 120 people.

Architect

Architect of the two buildings: Aurovilian
Anupama Kundoo
Entrance hall design: Roger Anger

Contact:
acur@auroville.org.in

Earlier Reception desk, now a small browsing centre at the Auroville Centre for Urban Research (ACUR), generally known as the Town Hall.

Building locations in the Town Hall area

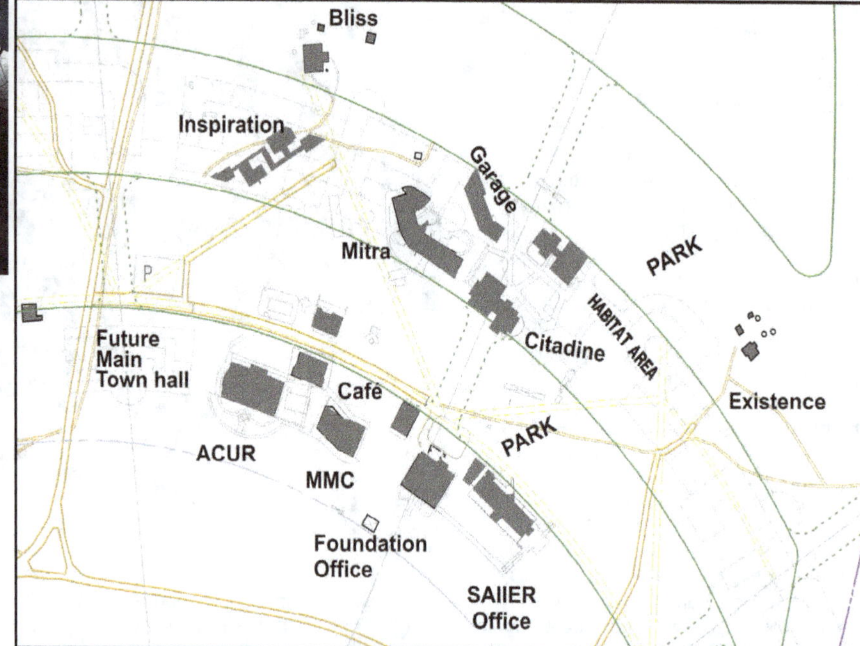

West end of Town Hall, with sculptures by Roger Anger

Previously Town Hall reception desk, now a small browsing centre offices; and elevated walkway

Various sections of the Town Hall complex by Anupama Kundoo, who based her designs on earlier sketches by Auroville's chief architect, Roger Anger.

Multimedia Centre

Le Morgan Café, and Multimedia Centre,
Multimedia Centre Auditorium

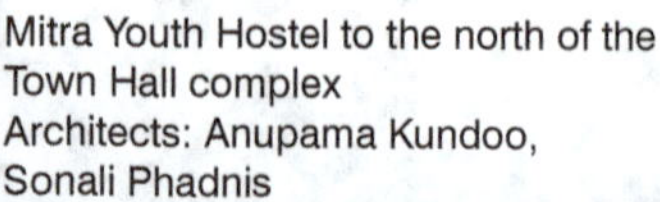

Mitra Youth Hostel to the north of the
Town Hall complex
Architects: Anupama Kundoo,
Sonali Phadnis

SAIIER*
*Sri Aurobindo International Institute for Educational Research

Financed by a Govt. of India grant and completed in 2013, the new SAIIER building is a G+2 structure with long, narrow form. Being an office building, it has been planned to have maximum daylight, natural ventilation throughout the year, plenty of space, and to be economical to run and maintain.

Of special interest, the south-west elevation has large sun shading screens to protect the interior from the afternoon sun. Complementing this, the narrowness of the form and higher ceilings achieve good ventilation, which is further enhanced by the work spaces being open-planned without walls, except for a couple of executive offices and the meeting room. The veranda on the eastern and western facades acts as an expansion of the office space, and also provides shade to the walls, further reducing the glare.

Although the building has space for rotating exhibitions of Auroville artists, some elements of the architecture can be seen in their own right as 'built in' art, like – for example - the window designed by Auroville artist Michele, and the big painted wall at the reception by Veronique. Another impressive 'art' feature is the central spiral staircase in the 10m. high reception lounge, with local wood flooring contrasting beautifully with natural white granite in the office spaces.

Final noteworthy features are: (1) the conference hall on the first floor has been made accessible by an outside ramp, making the building completely barrier-free, (2) all the neem trees in front of the building, although partly hiding the facade, have been retained to give shade to the front pathway area, and (3) the building's wastewater treatment plant has been integrated into the landscape in such a way that it acts as one of the aesthetic features of the garden area.

SAIIER building from outside and within inside

Architect: Sonali Phadnis

Arka

Arka is a research project of the Sri Aurobindo International Institute of Educational Research (SAIIER) constructed over the period 2002 to 2010. It is an innovative social project which wants to redefine the concept of ageing as described by the Mother, covered in a book on the subject titled "Eternal Youth".

Arka is a holistic centre creating an environment in which seniors can dedicate themselves to the inner work pertaining to their particular stage in life, while sustaining a healthy, balanced and harmonious lifestyle. Arka aims to keep people healthy and active as long as possible.

Towards this end, the public building facilities include a browsing service with internet and phone, a dining facility, a library, a multipurpose hall for yoga, dance, entertainment and other programmes, therapy rooms, and a beauty salon. The private area includes staff quarters, housing for residents, convalescence rooms for Aurovilians and Newcomers, guest rooms, laundry facility, garden with ponds and fruit trees, a walking track with gymnastic tool for mobility, 2- and 4-wheeler parking, with a coffee shop yet to be realized.

Architect: Dharmesh Jadeja (original concepts)

Institute for Integral Health

The mission of the Auroville Institute for Integral Health (AIIH) is to provide the community of Auroville with an effective health care system. To accomplish this task it has adopted an integral approach to the practice of medicine while considering the human being not as a "machine" but rather as a multi-dimensional entity – physical, emotional, mental and spiritual – and by utilizing the collaboration of different medical systems and traditions.Close to Auroville's Residential Zone and major public institutions, the AIIH occupies an area of approx 1.5 ha on the Crown Road next to Arka (which is dedicated to wellness and care of the elderly). The first phase (due to be finished in 2014) of approx 640 sqm plinth area (460 sqm carpet area) has been planned to accommodate a range of essential services, most of which have been temporarily housed in nearby Kailash.

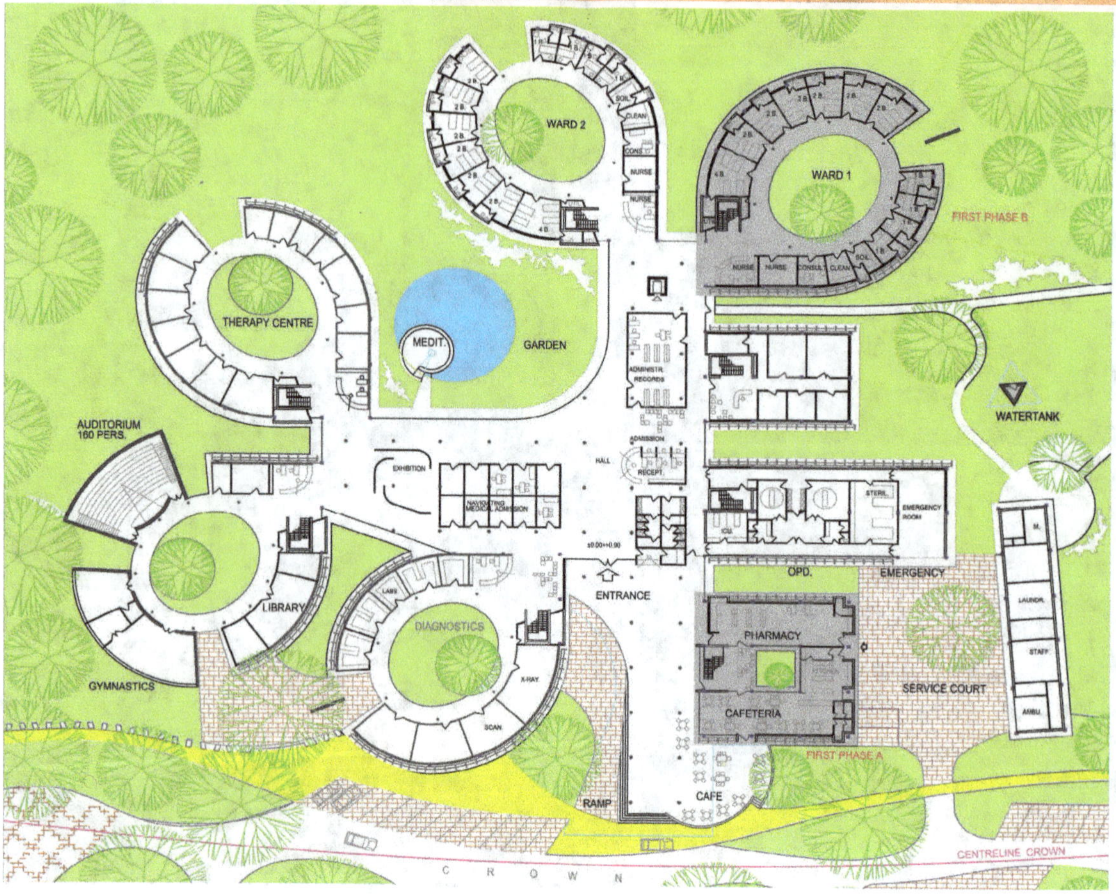

Architect:
Helmut Schmid

The Auroville Library

The new 630m² Auroville Library building located on the Crown Road near the Solar Kitchen, designed by long-time Aurovilian architect Suhasini Ayer, was completed in 2010 and has been operational since late 2011.

Essentially the building, which was constructed through a grant from the Central Government, is a framed structure (as per Tamil Nadu PWD regulations) and the campus will accommodate further buildings of ground + 2 to meet the needs of the city as it grows. It has been designed for an initial Auroville population of 5,000, in such a way as to provide ample book shelving space, office space for cataloguing books and book maintenance, a reference section with computerized browsing facility, tables for reading and laptop usage, and a small children's library, all in such a way as to provide climatic comfort without need for modulation using electrical / mechanical means. All infill walls are of rammed earth, and finishing materials used have as much as possible been taken from natural / local sources to minimise inclusion of industrial products with high embodied energy. Courtyards, transitional spaces and semi-covered spaces are shaded to allow for multiple usage; all trees with ecological / aesthetic value on site have been retained without damage during construction; and a few additional trees have been planted for further shading and aesthetic reasons.

The new building allows the Library to be more easily accessible to users thanks to its central location. It also provides more space for books and easier access to the collections, so represents a major improvement over the previous Library circumstances. The interior design and the equipment of the new building have been also completed thanks to a grant from the Central Government.

Architect: Suhasini Ayer-Guigan

Solar Kitchen

Located to the west of the Certitude-Matrimandir road, opp. the Kailash building, with seating capacity for 380, the Solar Kitchen, which was completed in 1998, is designed to provide meals for up to 1,000 Aurovilians and guests. The most interesting technological feature of the building is its roof-mounted 15-metre diameter (fixed spherical) solar concentrator.

The Auroville Guest Service office, an Auronet internet facility and a café are located on the roof.

The recently functional Prosperity Pour Tous facility, completed in 2006, is located close by, in the same compound.

Contact: Tel: 0413-2622197
solarkitchen@auroville.org.in

Architect: Suhasini Ayer-Guigan

Solar Kitchen, 1998

East side of the
Solar Kitchen, 2014

Pour Tous Distribution Centre

Located adjacent to the Solar Kitchen, the Pour Tous Distribution Centre – one of the "Prosperity Services" – has been acting as a distribution centre since 2006 for a wide range of food items, ready-made meals to take away and other goods supplied in kind (without any direct exchange of money, based on a cooperative participation) to Aurovilians, Newcomers and volunteers.

Inside the Prosperity Pour Tous facility, ▶ located in the Solar Kitchen area

Architect: Suhasini Ayer-Guigan
Prosperity Pour Tous complex entrance

SAIIER* Schools
*Sri Aurobindo International Institute for Educational Research

Contact: **Tel: +91-413-2622210, saiier@auroville.org.in**

Architect: Suhasini Ayer-Guigan

Kindergarten

Located at Centre Field, the Kindergarten (above) functions for children aged 3-7, dividing them into groups on the basis of age, affinity and ability. The teaching medium is English, but Tamil and French are also taught. Activities include those which develop manual skills, concentration and the beginnings of reading and writing. Teachers also try to cultivate in the children the habit of being quiet and relaxed.

Started in 1984, the Kindergarten today provides for nearly 50 children in four groups. About half are of Tamil origin, the remainder usually from some 10 other nationalities. The international coordinating team consists of half-a-dozen or more main teachers and assistant teachers plus 5 specialised teachers for music, Sanskrit song, swimming and body awareness.

Progress Landscape
(previously Last School)

Located near Aspiration community, the building is planned to be used as an educational facility dealing with landscaping.

After School
(previously "Sanskrit School")

The "After School" building (classroom, entrance and interior garden shown below) is used today for higher education, providing computer facilities, a library and classrooms for Aurovilian students.

Progress Landscape (previously Last School)

Architect: Roger Anger

Transition School

A school complex for approx 200 Auroville children aged 6-15. This is one of the larger elementary English medium Auroville schools, with 14 main classrooms + 5 smaller classrooms, a common hall, a crafts room and a video room set in extensive grounds. While a third of the students are Tamil, usually around 15 nationalities are represented. Some 25-30 Aurovilians assist in the teaching and coordination.

(Dates of completion for the various facilities are listed on page 155.)

Architects: Piero & Gloria Cicionesi

Transition School library

Future School

A relatively new school building, inaugurated in 2003, for the age group 15-19, at the entrance of Transformation community, it has special labs for physics, biology, chemistry and computer sciences. Students of the school can choose from a wide variety of languages and other subjects, and are also able to prepare for and take internationally recognised exams if they wish.

Two additional classrooms and 4 seminar rooms were added in 2005; a library building in 2012; and four additional classrooms in 2013.

Architects: Piero & Gloria Cicionesi

Future School's library of 7-8,000 books is primarily for the use of students and teachers of the school.

New Era Secondary School classrooms

Previously the Auroville Language Laboratory, the buildings are planned for use by New Era Secondary School (NESS) as a complex of classrooms.

Architect: Roger Anger

Super School building

What was known as Super School building is now allotted for eventual use by Deepam and for evening classes in Tamil, though before that it will be used by New Era Secondary School (NESS).

Super School

Architect:
Anupama Kundoo

The Pyramids

What was previously the Pyramid Art Centre has now been allotted to New Era Secondary School (NESS) for use as science laboratories, and to another user for science exhibitions.

Architect: Roger Anger

The present coordinating team includes a number of permanent full time teachers, and several others who come for specific classes.

As part of the educational approach, the school places special emphasis on artistic education, in addition to the usual formal curriculum. Subjects such as painting, music, dance, singing, drama and gardening are considered to be as important as the more traditional ones. It is also Deepanam's aim to have the four key languages mentioned by the Mother

Architect: Satprem Maini

implemented at all levels. With this in mind the older children study Tamil, Sanskrit, English and French, and the smaller ones are exposed to the same languages.

Deepanam School

The school started in May 2000, when a group of people experienced in education took over the premises of the former Mirramukhi School. After some changes, the school began operating in July 2000 with around 30 children aged from 2½ to 12 years, divided into 5 groups.

Last School

The Last School facilities needed to relocate to the Cultural Zone from their existing campus near Aspiration, and the design of the new buildings has now woven the various functions of the previous campus together. The Art Centre and the classrooms still have their own distinctive areas, pivoting around a two storey cylindrical block designed to house meeting and quiet spaces at the heart of the plan. The Art Centre comprises four interlocked spaces where art, sculpture and craft are taught and the central spine of the classroom area has been designed to exhibit the artwork of the students - so as they move throughout the day between each classroom they are immersed in an inspiring, ever-changing gallery of their own creations.
A water-body surrounds the classroom block, and it is an experiment to see if the level can be maintained through a combination of recycled grey water and the rainwater from the roofs.

Architects: David Nightingale & Ganesh Bala

Aikiyam School

Aikiyam is a day school in the New Creation settlement for more than 200 village children, where all tuition, educational supplies, nutritious snacks and mid-day meals are provided free of charge. The school's aim is to provide a high quality bilingual education in Tamil and English up to 8th standard, covering all standard academic subjects, computer training, art, crafts, physical education, and a wide variety of vocational options to prepare children for life in a rapidly changing world, while still maintaining contact with their Tamil cultural heritage. The school also has a programme for children with special needs. In April 2008 the school received provisional affiliation for a period of three years from India's Central Board of Secondary Education and is entitled to issue a recognized school leaving certificate. Students wanting to continue their academic studies may go to Auroville's New Era Secondary chool (NESS), a CBSE affiliated high school, or any other high school of their choice.

Architect: André Hababou

Udavi School

Located adjacent to Edayanchavadi village, Udavi School – which caters for children from the local villages – is trying to follow the guidelines on education laid down by the Mother and Sri Aurobindo, while taking the children up from 1st to 10th standard in preparation for their Government-held Matriculation examination at around the age of 17-18 years.

Architect: Poppo Pingel   Udavi School

La Piscine

La Piscine

La Piscine is a 25m swimming pool with changing rooms adjacent to New Creation Sports Ground.

Architects: Poonam, Shailaja   Nandanam

Nandanam Kindergarten and Crèche

Located in the area of Centre Field, Nandanam acts as second kindergarten for Auroville children aged 3 to 6 years. There is also a crèche facility for younger children which forms part of the complex.

Ilaignarkal Education Centre

Located north-west of the Town Hall. Runs an after-work school called The Heritage School for approx 40 young Auroville workers, providing functional literacy classes, vocational training and other further learning opportunities. The site also functions as a youth hostel for young people wanting to explore Auroville.

Architect: Suhasini Ayar-Guigan

Arka

ARKA is an innovative social project of Auroville which wants to redefine the concept of aging as described by the Mother. ARKA will create an environment in which the seniors can dedicate themselves to the inner work pertaining to their particular stage in life, while sustaining a healthy, balanced and harmonious lifestyle.

The concept of Arka comes from the belief that an enlightened society must provide for children and the elderly as well as for its intermediary majority population. The Arka project specifically addresses the following issues:

• In the coming years 10% of the total Aurovilian population will be aged over 65. Auroville's health facilities are not yet sufficiently developed to adequately meet the needs of such senior citizens.

• Currently the infrastructure in Auroville does not provide special facilities for elderly people or for handicapped individuals.

Architect: Dharmesh Jadeja

• Suitable roads, transport, safety, health and building specifications for geriatrics and others have not yet been developed.

To provide for the aging population a strong base is needed now. The steady growth and development of the Arka project itself will ensure a secure and progressive future for Auroville's senior citizens, enabling them to be receptive to the pressing forces of the new creation.

Contact:
Tel: 0413-2623799
Email: arka@auroville.org.in

Kuyilapalayam School
(associated with Auroville but not under SAIIER)

Located adjacent to Kuyilapalayam village, it provides education for nearly 900 pupils from the local villages in the Auroville area. The pupils who finish the 12th standard are able to go on to college directly.

Bommaiyapalayam School
(associated with Auroville but not under SAIIER)

A sub-school of the Kuyilapalayam School Trust, the school has 250 pupils in the age group 3 to 6, mainly from the local villages in the Auroville area. At the age of 10, the pupils go on to the main Kuyilapalayam School.

Architect: Werner Stoff

Pitanga Hall

In 1991 Pitanga opened its doors to Aurovilians who were willing to freely share their professional knowledge in aspects of health and culture. For this reason, Pitanga was built centrally, at the community of Samasti. The building consists of two large halls and six smaller rooms. These are placed intimately around a green courtyard with a pond and fountain.

Pitanga was named by its founders after a sweetly flowering Brazilian bush, the flowers of which bring peace and harmony. The name was found to also mean 'golden body' in Sanskrit.

Pitanga is open to both Aurovilians and guests. In the season from August to March, some thirty teachers offer a wide range of classes, from Yoga to Aikido, and from Chinese calligraphy to Salsa dance. Also, friends of Auroville from abroad, who are qualified teachers, are given opportunities to conduct courses and workshops.

To these activities are added Auroville art exhibitions and performances of music, dance and theatre. Sometimes performances are also given by promising artists from India or abroad.

Contact:
Tel: 0413-2622561
Email: pitanga@auroville.org.in

Architect: Rolf Redis

Auroville Health Centre

The Auroville Health Centre complex includes a handicapped children's day-care centre (Deepam), medical lab, X-ray facility and a pharmacy.

The Health Centre runs a programme of basic curative, preventive and rehabilitative services. Recognised as a Mini Health Centre by the Tamil Nadu State Government, it is equipped with basic medical facilities to serve the Auroville community as well as some 200 patients daily from the villages via its headquarters near Aspiration and its seven sub-centres. A team of 30 local women trained as village health workers by the Health Centre are active in 17 villages in the Auroville bio-region, providing first aid, home cures and basic health education.

Beginnings

The Auroville Health Centre traces its humble beginnings to 1969, when the Mother allocated Rs.5,000 to start a dispensary in a thatched hut in the Auroville area now known as Douceur. There were hardly any Aurovilians living in the area at that time, and the dispensary was created mainly to serve the villagers from nearby Kuyilapalayam village. It expanded rapidly, and by the end of 1973 a permanent structure, designed by Piero and Gloria Cicionesi, had been built with a major private donation plus funds from the Government of India and Auroville, and continued to add more buildings up to 1991. At present the Health Centre treats over 30,000 patients a year, 10% of whom are Aurovilians.

Contact: Tel: 0413-2622123
avhealth@auroville.org.in

Staff Quarters. Architect: Helmut Schmid ▶

(bottom right) Hospital extension building used by Deepam Day-Care Centre. Architect: Ajit Koujalgi

Health Centre main building Architects: Piero & Gloria Cicionesi ▼

Entrance hall

Quiet Healing Centre

Quiet Healing Centre, completed in 1997, is Auroville's main alternative health care facility, located in a beach-front compound approx 5 kms north of Pondicherry, half way to Auroville. The Centre offers a variety of therapies and also has a yoga/conference hall and guest facilities.

The land was previously owned by a family with close ties to the Sri Aurobindo Ashram, and the Mother occasionally visited the site. She is said to have remarked that a powerful healing energy was concentrated there. Many years later, one of the Mother's former secretaries was moved to help realise a place where this powerful healing energy could be utilised for all. Funds were raised, the land was acquired for Auroville, and construction of facilities began. The Centre opened in February 1997.

The healing work at Quiet is based on the understanding that humans are first and foremost spiritual beings seeking to express truth through the instrumentality of their mental, vital, and physical nature. Disharmonies occur as the more or less ignorant instruments deform the energies trying to manifest through them, and it is these disharmonies which we recognize as disease. The various (non-invasive) therapies offered at Quiet all seek, in one way or another, to address the patient's difficulties on an energetic level, which is the only level from which real healing can proceed. Each therapy honours and strives to work in harmony with the body's own deep wisdom. Each therapist recognises him- or herself as a humble tool of the indwelling Spirit – ultimately, the only Healer.

Accommodation

Two guest houses with a total of thirteen aesthetically pleasing and comfortably appointed double rooms are available for those wishing to stay at Quiet while taking therapy. The Quiet kitchen prepares three healthy vegetarian meals per day under carefully monitored hygienic conditions.

Contact:
Tel: 0413-2622329, 2646 or 3094
Email: quiet@auroville.org.in

Architect: Poppo Pingel, Quiet Guest House complex, with main building below

Yoga Hall and roofs of therapy rooms   Therapy Pool   Reception

Other buildings

Aurelec – Prayogashala

These buildings, the first designed by Poppo, were originally constructed by Aurelec Trust for their computer manufacturing business, but are now managed by a new Trust - ADPS Trust - as a business centre, housing a number of commercial units and services from Auroville and elsewhere. There is also a widely used cafeteria in the compound.

Contact:
Email: adps@auroville.org.in
Aurelec Cafeteria & Art Gallery, Tel: 0413-2622416 / 93 / 94

Architects: Poppo Pingel, Rehman, Suhasini Ayer-Guigan, Ajit Koujalgi

Aurelec Cafeteria & Art Gallery

Aureka

Aureka is a metal workshop which manufactures the Auram Presses used to produce Compressed Earth Blocks (CEBs). These blocks are environmentally-friendly and cost-effective and lend themselves to a variety of creative and aesthetically pleasing effects.

Resulting from increased world awareness of cost- and energy-effective materials, CEBs are now considered to be one of the first choices among appropriate building materials.

Located near Aspiration, Aureka undertakes also all types of metal work. Illustrated on the left is the main administrative building, and below the Auram Press 3000.

Tel: 0413-2622278 / 134
Email: aureka@auroville.org.in

Architect: Poppo Pingel

Auram Press 3000

Lines of Force

The so-called Lines of Force (LOF) buildings are seen as dynamic elements of the town layout, curved like the outward radiating arms of a galaxy and varying in height. They are intended as experiments in high-density living, each LOF being expected to have a different design and be composed of one large building or several interconnected structures.

Their aim will be to try to promote a more communal lifestyle. The first building (illustrated below), named 'Progress', represents the first phase of the first LOF.

Architect: Dominique Dube

Water Tower

Located near Prayatna community, the 26m high tower provides water to a number of nearby communities via its 130,000 litres capacity overhead tank (with underground reserve of 200,000 litres). The Water Tower was completed in 1998.

Architect: Helmut Schmid

Vérité Integral Learning Centre

Space for conferences and seminars. Completed 2005

Architects: David Nightingale & Ganesh Bala
Contact: ganesh_bala@hotmail.com

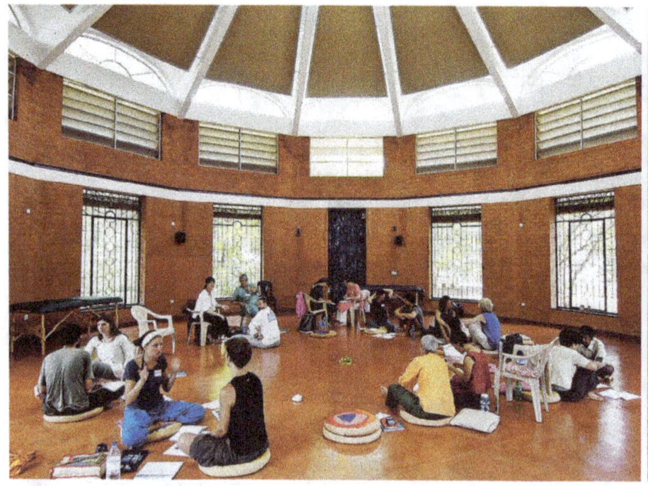

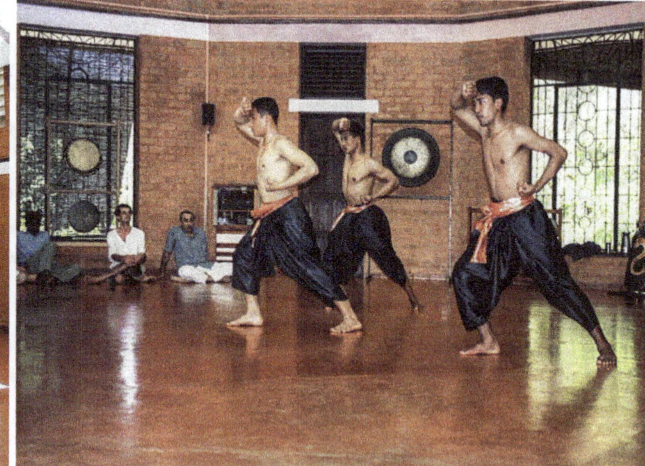

Vérité Yoga Hall

Architect: Raman

The Yoga Hall in Vérité settlement was completed in 1997 and offers space for yoga classes, conferences, seminars and other community needs.

Contact:
Vérité Community
Tel: 0413-2622045, e-mail: verite@auroville.org.in

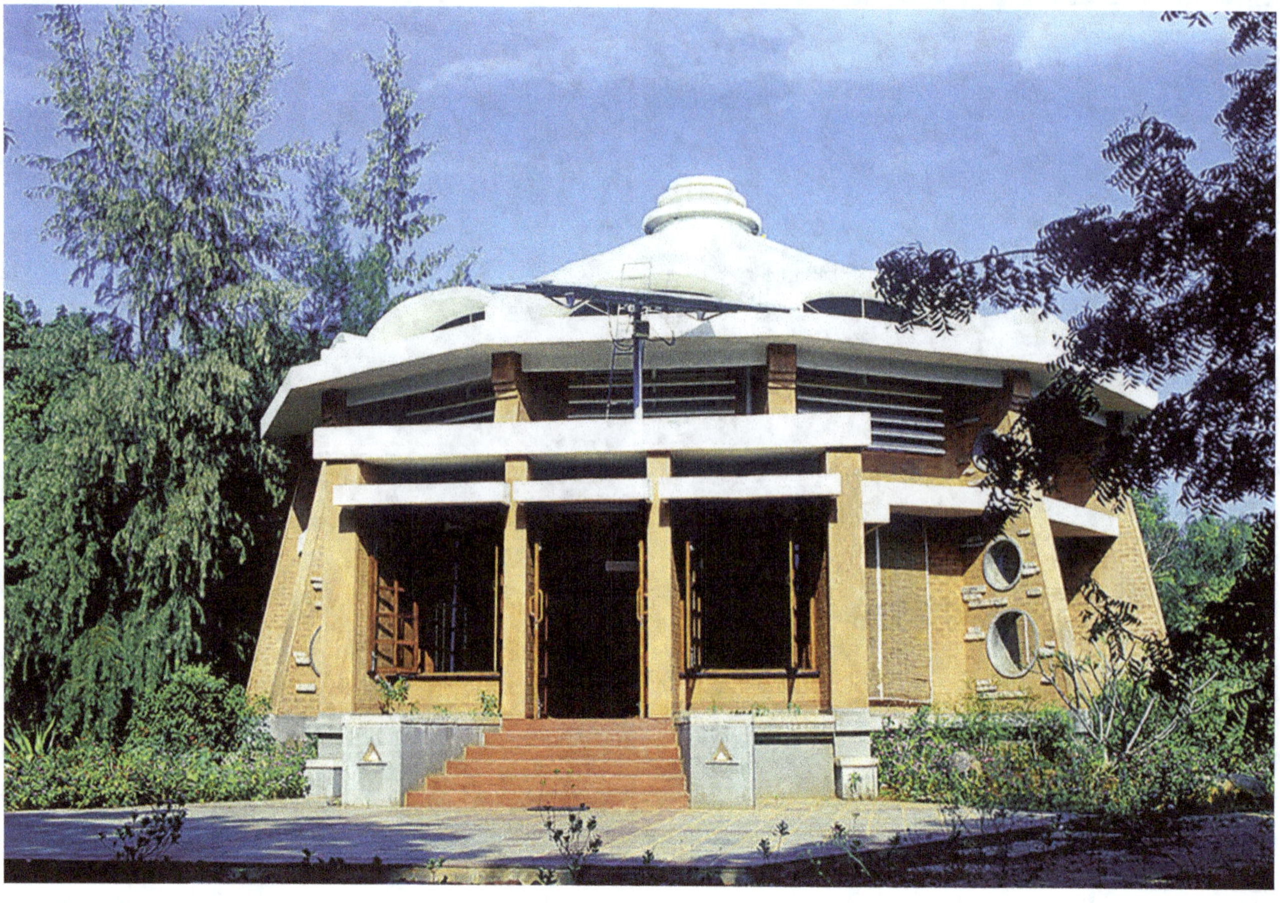

Road Service

Sited at the heart of the Service Area, close to the junction of the Kuilapalayam-Edayanchavadi stretch of tar road opposite the BSNL Telephone Exchange building, where the dirt road joins to Certitude and beyond, the Road Service complex, completed in late 2012, has been designed to house facilities for all Auroville's present and future road building and maintenance needs. These range from establishment, modification and maintenance of dirt roads, tracks and pathways, including cycle paths, to the laying of more permanent paved-block stretches of road such as the Crown Road and radials (no tar roads are presently planned in Auroville, due to pollution concerns). For these purposes, in addition to some office space the complex houses machinery such as tractors, trailer, water tanks, tippers, plate rammers, a JCB, road roller, mixer machine, and a paver machine.

The unit works exclusively for Auroville and takes on no outside work.

Contact: Tel: 2622844
roadservice@auroville.org.in

Architect: Sonali Phadnis

Guest Houses

Architect: Poppo Pingel

Afsanah Guest House

One of Auroville's major guest houses, located to the north-west of the Auroville township in the area of Kottakarai, Afsanah Guest House offers a range of variously priced high quality accommodation, plus availability of meals. The guest house is one of Auroville's best known and long established facilities. Set in quiet and pleasantly landscaped surroundings in Japanese style, it has been providing a high standard of comfort and service since 1989.

Presently the guest house has accommodation for up to 28 people in a variety of single, double and multiple units.

Tel: 0413-2622048
Email: afsanah_gh@auroville.org.in

Dining Hall at Afsanah guest house

Centre Guest House

Auroville's best known long-established guest house, providing a variety of accommodation and food for up to 50 people, located at Centre Field. Evolving from the late seventies onwards, various architects have been involved in this complex. The guest house particularly offers a good opportunity for guests to meet Aurovilian residents, who regularly take lunch there.

Tel: 2622155
Email: centreguesthouse@auroville.org.in

Architect: Suhasini Ayer-Guigan

Samasti Guest House

A medium sized guest house located in Samasti community, near Pitanga, providing single and double rooms.

Tel: 0413-2622105

Atithi Griha

(See p.68.)

A guest house located in the Bharat Nivas compound, which provides single, double and dormitory accommodation in a building which incorporates some antique woodwork and is built on the lines of traditional Indian architecture.

Tel: 0413-2622283

Samasti guest house

Architects: Ajit & Ratna Koujalgi

Gaia's Garden Guest House

Gaia's Garden is an ecological settlement trying to live in harmony with nature.
The guest house was completed in 1997 and can accommodate 12 people.

Tel: 0413-2622739 or 2622720
Email: kireet@auroville.org.in

Gaia's Garden guest house

Builder : Kireet

Fraternity Guest House

A small guest house located in Fraternity settlement, near the Aurelec compound.

Tel: 0413-2622789

Architect: Poppo Pingel
Fraternity guest house

Profiles of architects

Roger Anger

French-born architect Roger Anger, who was responsible for putting forward the concept of the Auroville Galaxy Town Plan and the design of the Matrimandir, the Amphitheatre and a variety of other significant structures and buildings in Auroville, was chosen by the Mother to be the Chief Architect of Auroville at the time of Auroville's conception in 1965.

Matrimandir

Matrimandir and Amphitheatre

Educated and trained in France, after leaving the 'Beaux Arts' Roger began to construct a number of buildings which were soon perceived to be far ahead of their time. This immediately identified him as one of France's most avant garde and promising architects. Talking about this phase of his life Roger says, "My inspiration was Le Corbusier. He was a genius in his use of form. He did not look to the past, only to the future, and he was single-minded, bold in his conceptions. He could be called the father of the new architecture in the same way as Picasso was the father of the modern movement in painting."

The next big step came for Roger in August 1965 when the Mother, to whom he had been closely connected for a number of years, called on him to take up the challenge of Auroville. Roger remembers, "At the beginning we were a very small city design team but we were full of enthusiasm and energy: the dream was 'pure', full of joy, and it was wonderful because Mother wanted Auroville to be a place of continual experimentation.

Last School

Mother did not want Auroville to be a city catering to the ease of its inhabitants: it was to be a place to develop their consciousness. Above all, it was to be an experiment in a new form of collectivity. This is why, although I have been obliged to design some, I am against the idea of individual houses, gardens, land in Auroville, for they do not at all correspond to the spirit of the experiment, which wants to express something beyond the personal. How far can a planner create collectivity? He can help, but finally, without a change of consciousness in the inhabitants, there will be no collectivity, however well planned the city may be."

Pyramids Arts Centre, Aspiration

Residence, Auromodèle,
Sculpture by Roger Anger

Switching from the broad concept to specifics, Roger goes on: "When I designed Last School it was a revolution in terms of the architectural concepts of that time because of the freedom of its shape. While we used there some indigenous technologies, like bamboo, generally I have worked with ferrocement, which, in its plasticity, represents the creativity of the city. I started working with it in Auromodèle, the community which was to be the first experiment in the creation of the city. I made a design for 2,000 inhabitants with integrated houses and gardens in a collective environment. While it was not adopted, something of that environment remains."

Although Roger temporarily severed his practical connection with Auroville in 1974 to avoid getting drawn into a power struggle which was then enveloping the township and its residents, he always remained connected. Regular visits over the years helped him keep pace with Auroville's development, then in 1988 - coinciding with the passing of the Auroville Foundation Act - he decided to become more directly involved again. Commenting on his decision that year, he said: "During Mother's time I attempted to push towards the imaginary, the future, but following her departure (in 1973) it was no longer possible." Then later, "My role, I feel, is to push the future forward."

On Auroville he has said more specifically: "The difficulty is how to find the exact balance that includes nature and habitat. The differences in density, the integration of space in which one communicates, in which one feels freed from the heaviness of buildings, this has never been attempted in the world; one has never made an experimental city of this nature. Auroville, on the level of urban research, involves a search for different types of zones - low, medium and high; a city that can be lived and experienced through one's eyes, incorporating perspectives, moments that surprise you and catch your attention, others that convey a feeling of rest and tranquillity, others a feeling of surprise."

"When it came to planning the city, Mother put pressure upon us to make the original concept more and more dynamic. In fact, as an architect I have simply been an instrument to express her vision. Few people understand this. Sometimes I have agonised over a difficulty for many years, then, suddenly, as I finish a drawing, I know I have the solution. It's because I have opened to her, I have made the connection."

Roger Anger has already made a major contribution on a practical, material and aesthetic level to the Auroville of today, but perhaps more importantly he has also inspired other architects and designers to expand their personal horizons, and to seek for the inspirational and beautiful in their work. His own bold thrust towards - and exploration of - the future has certainly been his personal hallmark.

(Roger Anger passed away in Paris aged 84 on 15th January 2008.)

Residence, Auromodèle

Entrance to After School

Auroville Language Laboratory,
Architect Roger Anger

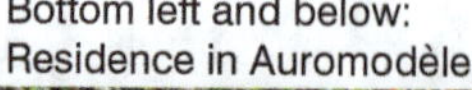

Bottom left and below:
Residence in Auromodèle

Piero & Gloria Cicionesi

What was your background?
We were both qualified architects from the University of Firenze in Italy. We received training in Finland for 2 years, and also worked in Italy for 6 years.

Through your work, what are you trying to find, or express?
The more the years accumulate, and one can see things in a larger perspective, the more we have today the feeling that quality references for architecture are similar to qualities attributed to human beings, seen from the outside as well as from the inside. We think here of qualities defined by adjectives like sober, honest, correct, simple, sincere, intelligent, amiable, bright, elegant, wise, solid, alive, dynamic. As designers and sadhaks of the integral yoga we try to express these attributes through our work.

When we arrived here in 1968, we were struck by the beauty and fine detailing of the Golconde building of the Sri Aurobindo Ashram in Pondicherry. The fact that the construction of this building was almost daily followed by the Mother, has been for us both the main force and inspiration to participate - with many other Aurovilians - in the construction of Matrimandir.

For more than 20 years, from 1971 onwards, we followed, designed, organised, oversaw, and solved the details of the work pertaining to the construction of the Matrimandir, starting from the laying of the foundations to the erection of the structure, the triangular space frame, and the finishing of the Inner Chamber, until finally in 1992 the focused sun rays started to shine on the crystal globe inside the Chamber.

Family or individual residences:
Aspiration community for 80 people + community kitchen (1970-72)
Auroson's Home, Certitude (1969-70)
New Community I, Certitude (1976-77)
New Community II, Certitude (1977-79)

Auroson's Home - first house in Certitude settlement

New Community building, Certitude

Transition School campus

New Community III apartments, Certitude (1977-78)
Cluster of 3 houses, Certitude (1972-73)
Shyamsunder house, Certitude (1975-76)
Andy's house, Certitude (1975)

Navoditte's house, Certitude (1976)
Ed & Mauna's house, Forecomers (1983-84)
Pierre-Charles' house, Dana (1992)
Rika's house, Certitude (1992-93)
Ilse's house, Gaia's Garden (1998)

Buildings of public interest:
Health Centre, Aspiration, 1st phase 1971-73, 2nd phase 1990-91
Gymnasium dome, Certitude (1987)

Residential house in Certitude

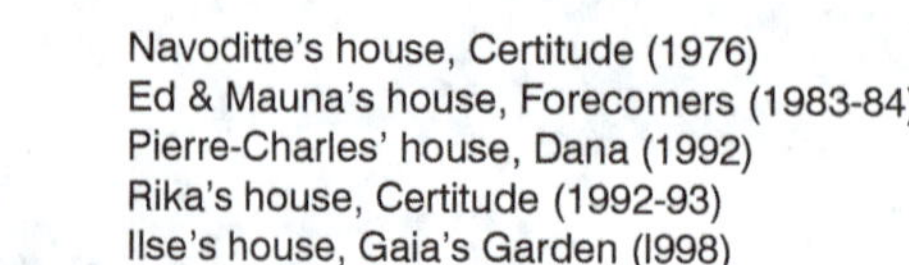

As part of Transition School campus:
Small Classrooms and common hall (1985)
Studios and Workshops (1987)
Library and Classrooms (1996)
Dining Hall and Body awareness hall -
gymnasium (1999)
Art and Craft Building and additional
classrooms (2004-2005)
Computer room and administrative room
(2006-2009)

Others
Music Centre - Cultural Zone (project only)
Unity Pavilion - 2001, International Zone

Contact: piero@auroville.org.in

Transition School campus

André Hababou

What was your background?
I did my training at 'Beaux Arts' in France, and came to Auroville in 1968 at the age of 26. Mother asked me to work with Roger Anger in the Office of Architecture, which I did for many years. It was a very special period for me, a time of grace. The atmosphere was delightful, and very creative, thanks to the talents of Roger, who also had the power to bring all the people to work together, guided by the influence of the Mother. At the time there were no disagreements amongst Aurovilians about the town, the zones, or the Matrimandir; whether to have discs, petals, etc. Mother was there, and everybody was at the right place doing the right thing. I learned a lot and attained a certain maturity. I am grateful to Roger and Mother.

What projects have you been responsible for?
- Centre for Research in Communication and Publication (CRCP), Fraternity;
- Surrender community - a residential collective housing project;
- the Pavilion of Tibetan Culture in the International Zone;
- Shradhanjali & Auromode commercial units, both in the Industrial Zone;
- the school at New Creation.

Through your work, what are you trying to find or express?
I try to express beauty and harmony, which is automatically linked with functionality.

Which of your works best expresses your vision or philosophy?
Auromode factory and my own residence in Auromodèle, because in both cases I didn't have to make any concession to clients.

Centre for Research in Communication & Publication

New Creation Bilingual School

Auromode office buildings

Surrender settlement

Please give some overview of the evolution of your work, and milestones on the way.
When I came to Auroville, everything was new here. We didn't have any experience about the climate for instance. The materials for building were very poor. Slowly, after committing many mistakes, we progressed.

Personally, I progressed most when I started working with models in 3 dimensions.

Which architectural project in Auroville do you appreciate most?
The Matrimandir, which is an expression of beauty and force.

Contact:
Andre Hababou,
Ph: 0413-2622193
Email: auromode@auroville.org.in
Web: www.auromode.com

Auromode office building

Pavilion of Tibetan Culture

Poppo Pingel

Born in 1942. Apprenticeship in carpentry, then studied architecture in Münster and Aachen, Germany. Since many, many years, has also been partially engaged in exploring "reverse architecture" – through archaeological rescue excavations, documentation and research in Auroville.

Fraternity workshops, 1973

Handmade Paper Workshop, 1973,
Aspiration settlement

When did you come to Auroville?
In1968, for the inauguration of Auroville, as the German delegate.

Nature of work in Auroville?
Experimental village houses with rammed earth 1970-1979; residences, workshops and guest houses in Auroville; Udavi School 1993; Natural Healing Centre at Quiet 1997; Afsanah Guest House, Kottakarai, 2003.

Please give some overview of the evolution of your work; some milestones on the way.
Coming to Auroville in 1970, the social aspects of architecture were predominant for me - village house experiments, mass village houses in rammed earth, individual low-cost houses, ample use of wood (tropical timber) and cement plus asbestos sheets, the latter without questioning at the time.

Later I began to question the reason and essence of architecture due to cultural collisions of different architectural approaches in Auroville.

In the late 1970s, due to cement shortage after the oil crisis (1973), I began looking into alternative, traditional building techniques and methods (mud, lime, vaults and domes).

In the early 1990s, my work was strongly influenced by the growing environmental awareness, *baubiological** and sensory issues plus physiological concerns in architecture. These included health hazards through industrial building materials, electro-smog, the blind use of industrial synthetic building products monotonously applied, and the waste and misuse of natural resources.

Through your work what are you trying to find or express?
Being brought up in traditional carpentry, I wish to see structural clarity in built form, simplicity in design and details, clear distinct visibility of building elements (all exposed, nothing hidden), and the harmonious composition of building materials in response to their nature.

It is important to see the integration of multiple aspects of architecture in creating a more harmonious whole, involving the landscape (environment), buildings, biological factors (health and well-being), the social dimension (people and their habits), and traditional craftsmanship (ancient building wisdoms).

My attempt is to go beyond the relativity of fashion-bound architecture through the subtlety of proportions, space formation, combinations of distinct building materials, their surfaces and textures, into something which is beyond style or fashion, something which does not cry for attention, which is timeless (always known but hidden) and universal, something of another dimension; a flowing of peace, serenity, play and

* *Baubiology, or "Building Biology", refers to the relationship between buildings and life.*

House in Certitude, 1983

Fraternity guest house, 1978

beauty together, where the mundane and the sacred lose their distinct separateness.

What I have briefly expressed above is not the exposition of an individual architectural philosophy, but rather a vision and the present result of an evolving contact with the ever-changing world of space and matter, its natural conditions and consequences, its relativities, and its ever time-bound demands for absoluteness. It is a search, an aspiration, and at the same time a dedication to the Infinite.

Which of your works best expresses your vision and approach?
Fraternity workshops, 1973; Franz' house and adjacent guest house, 1978; Certitude house, 1980; Jacques Verre's 'Shamiyana', 1984; Afsanah Guest House, 2002.

Fraternity workshops, 1973

Residence

Mukuduvidu, residences and office, 1992

Yantra, workshop, 1999

Residential building, Kottakarai, 2006

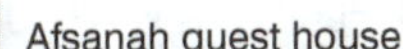

Afsanah guest house   Architect: Poppo Pingel

Peter Anderschitz

Since childhood I know of two passions where I can totally forget myself: designing spaces and dancing spaces.
Both are about harmony and beauty, about rhythm and resonance, both nourishing each other.

My 'profession', however, was to become an architect, urban-environmental planner and city-zen-builder, my chosen creative way of failing and soaring, the most amazing challenge to live and express integral beauty and harmony in this world.

Born in post-war Berlin, I grew up in a divided city, nation, culture. I studied architecture and urban planning at the Technical University Berlin, where in 1968 I got a diploma with O.M.Ungers, concluding with a thesis which was to become a radical critique of the established role and self-image of the architect in society.
I began to understand that my longing for beauty and harmony was not to be an exclusive one, but was to embrace all life, and that I had always been searching for that unifying essence in everything, for a spiritual grounding.

My 'career' therefore began quite experientially, as a taxi driver, living in communes, traveling to new horizons, always keeping myself open for the unexpected. And so I discovered Sri Aurobindo's work, which resulted in my reaching Mother India, meeting the Mother, seeing that strikingly radiating model of her dream city-with-a-soul, touching the red soil of that promised land, coming home. Here, in that laboratory of the future, the real journey could begin. This was in 1971/73.

Residence at Felicity settlement

Since then I have been working in the fields of housing, urban-environmental planning, international networking, land art, and lately in 'open space' participatory planning exercises, getting involved in various activities where integration, that 'unifying essence, has a chance to manifest:

In the 1970s, after working in 'Auroville's Future' planning office, being there temporarily side-tracked for far-away Indian steel town projects, I engaged myself in Auroville's Land Service for infrastructural integration, later designing a first urban housing cluster at Samasti and an individual residential compound at Felicity near Auromodele. But what about the city?

In 1989, quite unexpectedly, a stronger heartbeat called me beyond the already shaking Iron Curtain to present Auroville at the 'Prague Assembly of Architects & Planners for Ecology, Peace and Social Development'; then to Berlin, both becoming living encounters with 'nation soul' when she is cracked open the most. Fate?

It meant shuttling between Auroville and Berlin for a while, here getting engaged in urban planning essays, especially for the International Zone, and there closely experiencing a city in search of a new form and identity.

Today after having experienced Auroville's various exercises in non- planning, master planning, participatory planning, open planning, and witnessing a large variety of interesting architectural experiments coming up, most of them still out of sync with the needed urban context, I have finally formulated my concrete dreams for the next future:
- collaboration: expanding participatory planning processes, including the way of the Dreamcatchers, which opens up a new quality of collaboration and consensus emerging from inner silence
- planning: 'grounding' the urban vision by allowing the spirit of the 'Galaxy' urban design concept to resonate with the land and the people
- architecture: applied research in lightweight, adaptable, co-operative housing and living
- land art: creating experiential spaces for and with the 'youth that never ages'.

www.auroville.org, home, society, profile.
Mobile: 948 848 3348

Ajit & Ratna Koujalgi

When did you come to Auroville?
Ajit lived here from 1971-78 and 1987 till now; Ratna from 1987 till now.

Background, or some info on your training?
Ajit - studied architecture at School of Planning and Architecture in New Delhi; Ratna - studied at University of Hannover, Germany.

Some description of the nature of your work?
Interpretation of basic traditional architectural patterns to suit modern needs. Involvement in Pondicherry; protection of architectural heritage of the old town and restoration of old buildings.

Through your work, what are you trying to find, or express?
Searching for a 'timeless' architecture which is beyond the fads and doesn't struggle to be 'new' and 'inventive' for the sake of being so. Looking for an 'egoless' architecture as a balance to the ego-driven contemporary modern architectural movement.

Which of your works best expresses your vision, or philosophy?
Our own house in Samasti, as well as the pediatric clinic behind the Health Centre near Aspiration; also the extension of the École Française d'Extrème Orient and the Hotel de l'Orient in Pondicherry.

Deepam, Health Centre Pediatric Clinic

Please give some overview of the evolution of your work; milestones on the way.
(Ajit) I started my career with Aurofuture in 1971 and participated in several outside projects, like preparing master plans for steel towns in Salem, Kudremukh. I then worked in Germany from 1978 to 1986 and took the opportunity to critically evaluate what I had done till then, meanwhile using the university library and new professional

opportunities to re-educate myself. I got interested in environmental activism, the study and preservation of traditional built-forms, the essence of cities, etc, and came to know works of Christopher Alexander and Jeffrey Bawa, which have shaped our practice.

Contact: ajit@auroville.org.in

Residence at Samasti

Helmut Schmid

Before coming to Auroville in 1979 I was working for 10 years in a professional environment in Stuttgart, Germany, planning and designing Universities and Medical Schools.

Here I am involved in architectural designs and construction, mainly of institutional buildings.

Building design should not put the designer's personality in the foreground. Louis Kahn says "the architect's greatest worth is in the area where he can claim no ownership – the part that doesn't belong to him is his most precious". Looking in this direction the exploration of the creative process becomes a very exciting and rewarding experience.

"Uncompromising rules, robust and varied rhythmic expression, distinctiveness of melodic line, clarity and harshness of harmonies, trenchant radiation of textual hues, last but not least simplicity and transparency of the musical tapestry as well as firmness of the formal structure" – that's what Igor Stravinsky tried to achieve in his musical compositions. In my view it would also describe good architecture.

But architectural structures – however fine they may be – have only a limited value without their context.

To supply this context to architects working in Auroville a clear and systematic planning approach is required, based on an overall vision of the whole city in all its complexity of life, as well as an effective decision-making structure.

Only through this will we be able to realize "the city the earth needs".

Contact: Tel: 0413-2622149

Savitri Bhavan, entrance building

Grace settlement, apartment buildings

Water tank in Residential Zone

Dehashakti School Sports Complex, Table Tennis Hall

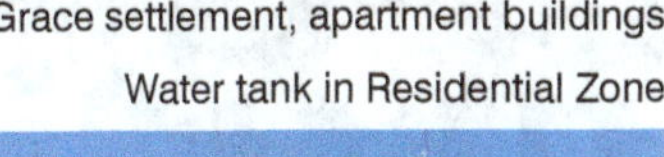

Suhasini Ayer-Guigan

Background, or some info on your training?
Suhasini Ayer-Guigan is a graduate of "Delhi School of Planning and Architecture"; living in Auroville since 1985, and one of the co-founders of the "Auroville Centre for Scientific Research", an organisation dedicated to research and experimentation in the field of appropriate building materials and technologies, water management, renewable energy and solar passive / climatic architecture and sustainable urban planning.

Some description of the nature of your work?
I head the "Auroville Design Consultants", the Planning and Design wing of this organization, and have designed and implemented over 50+ projects in India in the last 25+ years. Achievements include being a co-recipient of the Hassan Fathy Award for 'Architecture for the Poor' in 1992; being co-nominated for the Aga khan award in 1992; and being a recipient of the Design Share Award for educational buildings in 2003 and 2005. My specialities include:

● Institutional buildings like exhibition spaces, information centres, international and CBSE schools, hospitals and office buildings

● Hospitality projects – eco-resorts and spas
● Mixed and gated housing projects, multi-family homes, apartments and private homes
● Planning for sustainable land-use and urban planning for townships, housing and rehabilitation projects.

What are the guiding principles of the Auroville Design Consultants?
● Beauty and aesthetics in the built and natural environment, which are essential for healthy living. Minimalism is an integral part of designing to create simple and elegant forms in keeping with the sustainable and green building practices.
● The user/developer is part of the design team and not just a client. We seek active and informed participation with our clients.
● The planning and design should be most appropriate to the context – site conditions, function, climate, building materials and technology, ease of execution, cost effectiveness and environmental responsibility.

Contact:
Suhasini Ayer-Guigan
+91 413 262 2784, +91 94431 62784
www.aurovilledesign.com
suhasini@auroville.org.in

Residence house

Visitors Centre

Kindergarten

Bommaiyapalayam Kindergarten

Centre Guest House extension

Solar Kitchen

Rolf Redis

When did you come to Auroville?
In April 1986, after living in the Sri Aurobindo Ashram for 3 years.

Background, or some info on your training?
I worked with Pierre Elouard during the first two years of my stay in Auroville, and afterwards with nearly all the architects here.

Some description of the nature of your work?
As builder I have done:
With Poppo: Udavi School and Quiet Healing Centre complex.
With Helmut, Health Centre Staff Quarters, Arati water tank for Residential Zone.
With Ajit, Health Centre Children's Home and Bommaiyur toy factory, Kottakarai.
With Suhasini, Claude & Abha's extension in Dana.

With Anupama: Pierre's house in Petite Ferme and Juanita's House (along with Peter Anderschitz for concept).
With Vishwa: William Netter's House in Samasti.
With Piero & Gloria: Transition School (last 3 extensions) and High School.

As architect & builder:
Pitanga Hall, Samasti; Samasti Guest House (partly with Peter A.); Ursula's guest house in Samasti; Paul & Hatsu's house in Auromodèle; 2 houses in Arya; George's house in Shakti; an office in Shakti; Lumière extensions in Fraternity; and Invocation apartments.

Through your work, what are you trying to find, or express?
The Divine Will.

Which of your works best expresses your vision, or philosophy?
Invocation.

Please give some overview of the evolution of your work; milestones on the way.
The milestone in my learning process was the insight that all philosophies and ideologies, sometimes used by architects to justify their way of building, are basically there for the sole purpose of hiding one's own shortcomings. Common sense is sometimes more helpful. After all, where are the ideologies and philosophies in a silent mind?

Which architectural projects in Auroville do you appreciate most?
The work of Piero and Gloria.

Pitanga Hall (all three photos)

Wastewater treatment plant for
Invocation settlement

Arati apartments   Invocation apartments

Mona Doctor-Pingel

Ever since my first visit in 1987 as a trainee, and later when I joined in 1990, Auroville has been and is my "play field", which allows me to constantly formulate and re-evaluate my ideas and ideals. It has supported my growth as an individual in multifarious activities which are synergistic with architecture.

Having studied architecture at the Centre for Environment and Planning (CEPT), Ahmedabad (1984-90), and having obtained a masters degree in Appropriate Technology from Flensburg University, Germany (1992-94), I have had an independent set-up in Auroville since 1995.

With a vibrant, constantly changing team of trainees, young architects and designers at STUDIO NAQSHBANDI, Auroville has given me the freedom to experiment and learn through planning from macro to micro, with stress on details, client interactions,

Architect's own Studio, Yantra, 2008

interior design and landscaping, as a holistic realization of the project; creating spaces that lead to the well-being of the users, taking into account the five senses of the human being and activating them though architecture; including diverse aspects such as integrated water and energy management, use of locally available materials and techniques, as an intrinsic part of the design and not as fashionable add-ons. The inside-outside relationship does form an important part of my practice since I like to see the built form with its surroundings rather than in isolation.

Some of the projects executed include: exploration of domes and vaults in the tropical climate with the principles of Building Biology (Baubiologie) in communities like Yantra (4,500 sq.m. plot area, 1995-2008) and Udyogam (12,000 sq.m. plot area, 2002-2005); Deepanam School (2009-2012) buildings where tight budgets resulted in a search for light-weight roofing using GI sheets in innovative ways; Cottage restaurant (2007-2009) built in Pondicherry for Sri Aurobindo Ashram Trust, inspired by the iconic Golconde Dormitory and the Ashram Samadhi itself; Temple Tree Retreat, Guest House (2009-2011).

As part of "Dreamcatchers", an open source planning forum started in 2005, evolving an inclusive and creative process for Auroville's growth at all levels taught me that it is possible to find the Highest Common Denominator in a collective process rather than the Lowest Common Factor. I strongly believe that the consciousness one puts into the design and building process is bound to show in the end product.

A recent 2 year term (2010-2012) at L'avenir d'Auroville (Auroville's official Planning and Development body) allowed me to become aware of the difficulty of planning a city that is constantly in a flux. Auroville's planning presents one of the greatest challenges and privileges to live while developing a society that is based on nothing less than an evolution of consciousness to the next human species.

My current field of exploration also includes teaching (at various architecture schools and through hands-on workshops), writing (Monographs on Auroville Architects series – Poppo Pingel, Mapin Publishing House, 2012) and research (Energy Efficiency in Buildings under the joint Indo-US research programme : www.cberd.org/) mona@auroville.org.in   0413 - 2622900

Cottage Restaurant, 2009

Staff unit,
Udyogam, 2002

Class room,
Deepanam School,
2010
Aurosoya extension,
Udyogam, 2006

Avatar Syrups, Udyogam, 2005
Naturellement food processing unit,
Udyogam, 2005

Architect's own Studio, Yantra, 2008
Yantra, 1996

Yantra, 2000, Yantra, 2001

Temple Tree Retreat, Guest house, 2011

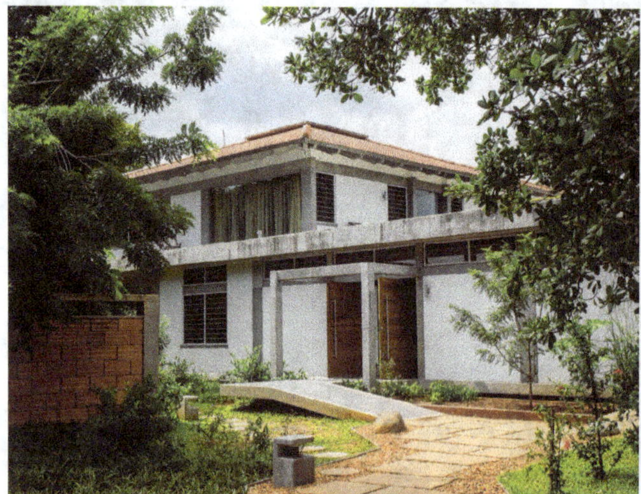

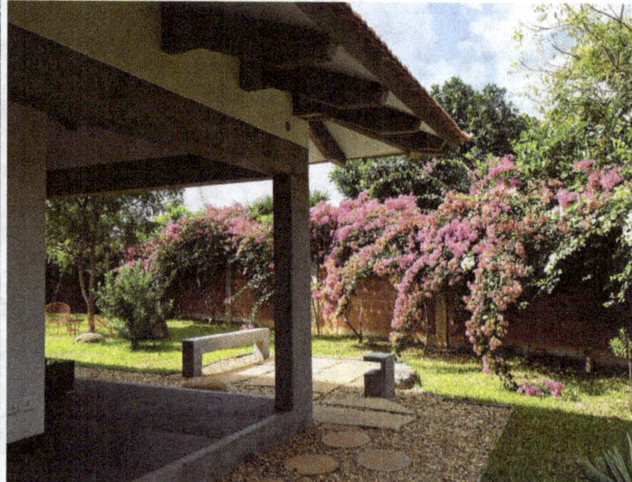

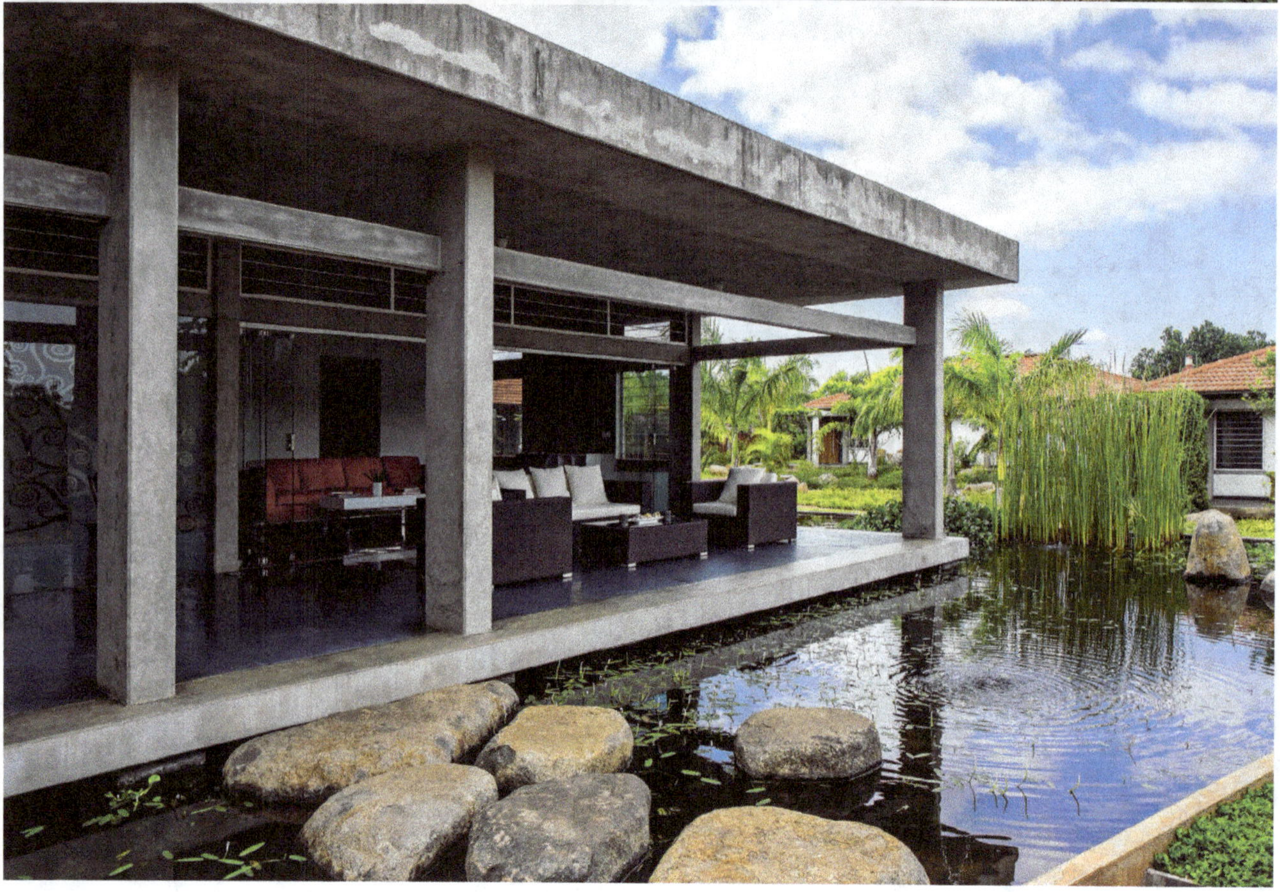

Guest house complex opposite Djaima community.

Satprem Maïni

Date of joining Auroville: End of August 1989.

Background:
1985: Architect DPLG graduation at the School of Architecture of Lyon, France.
1988: Postgraduate Diploma in Earth Architecture at the School of Architecture of Grenoble, France.
2000 onwards: Representative for Asia of the UNESCO Chair in Earthen Architecture.

Description of the nature of your work?
- Research and development of stabilised earth-based technologies and equipment for earth construction.
- Management of the AV Earth Institute.
- Dissemination of these technologies through publishing manuals and documents.
- Conducting training courses on earth technologies and arches, vaults and domes. More than 9,800 people from 78 countries have been trained)
- Giving consultancy within India and abroad.

What do you seek or express through your work?
This commitment leads me to work in various places around the world for the promotion of earth architecture and bringing awareness to people. I have worked in 36 countries up to now.
In general: to be a willing servitor of the Divine consciousness. In particular, to honour our Mother Earth by using its resources with a lot of respect and gratitude, and to help convey this message to the world; to get in touch with the Earth consciousness through matter.

Best works which express your vision?
- Deepanam (former Mirramukhi) School, Auroville.
- Vikas Community, Auroville.
- The dome of the Dhyanalingam Temple for Lord Shiva, near Coimbatore, and the Pyramid Temple to Sri Karneshwara

Realization

Nataraja, near Auroville.
Overview of the evolution of your work?
During my study of architecture I became interested in alternative building materials (such as second-hand wood) and also in the direct participation of people in the design and construction process.

In 1986, participated in construction of the 'House of 24 hours', which was built at Grenoble, France. I also worked for one month with Sister Emmanuelle in the slums of Cairo, Egypt.
In 1987, conducted a two-month training course and built a school in Somalia for UNESCO. Also conducted a one-month training course and built a demonstration house in the Ivory Coast.
In 1988, built the Exhibition Centre of the Royal Commission of Jubail and Yambu in Saudi Arabia. There followed a two-month training

working with rammed earth in Australia.
In 1989, conducted a one-month training course on compressed earth blocks in New Delhi. This was my first contact with India, during which I decided to join Auroville a few months later. I came to set up the former AVBC / Earth Unit, and built the Visitors Centre with Suhasini.

Between 1991 and 1997, designed and developed Vikas Community, Auroville. This project was a finalist for the 2000 World Habitat Award.
Between 1994 and 1995, built Mirramukhi (now Deepanam) School, Auroville.
In 1996, built a demonstration project for UNCHS/Habitat at the 1996 City Summit in Istanbul in two weeks.
During 1997, was lecturing, by invitation, in earth and appropriate building technologies in Brazil for three months.
In 1998, built with an 18-man team a disaster-resistant house at New Delhi in 66 hours.

In winter 1998-1999, directed the construction of the 22.16 metre diameter dome of the Dhyanalingam Temple near Coimbatore.
This dome of about 570 tons was built free-spanning in 9 weeks using unskilled labour.

After the Gujarat earthquake in 2001, I spent nearly six months helping, at regular intervals, with the construction of several thousand houses and Community Centres, the construction of demonstration

houses, and conducting various training programmes and evaluating the work of the Catholic Relief Services.

In winter 2003-2004 I was asked by the Development Authority of Riyadh, Saudi Arabia, to build a mosque in the heart of the city. This 435 sq.metre mosque was built in 7 weeks using about 75 semi-skilled masons and 150 unskilled labourers together with 5 assistants from the Auroville Earth Institute. In 2010 this project won first prize in "Prince Sultan Bin Salman Awards for Urban Heritage".

1998-2005 saw me involved in the construction of several vaults and domes of various shapes and spans for buildings in Auroville; cost effective houses; our training centre, etc.

After the tsunami of 2004, I was involved in the design of various projects for the reconstruction of affected areas and the construction of a tsunami house, the design of which won first prize in a national contest. I signed for the Auroville Earth Institute a 'Memorandum of Understanding' for the construction of various Technology Demonstration Units in several districts of Tamil Nadu. The first one was completed near Auroville at Bommaiyapalayam village, and acts as a community centre and office for the village. Another MoU was signed with UNDP in 2006 for continuation of transfer of technology.

2006 saw realisation of the nearby Sri Karneshwara Nataraja temple, which combines for the first time Egyptian culture and Hindu culture with a pyramid to house Lord Shiva Nataraja.

Architectural projects you most appreciate in Auroville?
Above all the Matrimandir. Also projects done by Helmut and Anupama are worth

Sri Karneshwara Nataraj Temple, Pudhukuppam

Vikas settlement apartments

mentioning for their integrity and quality.

Thirteen awards
2010 - First prize for Al Medy Mosque built in Riyadh, Saudi Arabia, given by Prince Sultan Bin Salman Award For Urban Heritage, Al-Turath Foundation, Saudi Arabia.
2006 - 1st prize in All India design competition "Multi hazard resistant shelter".
2005 - First prize in the national competition "Hazard-resistant house design contest".
2000 - "India Gold Star Award" and gold medal, by FFI - Excellence Award for personal achievement in his field of work.
- "Glory of India Award" and gold medal, by FFI - Excellence Award for Great Achievement and exploit in his field of work.

Interior of personal living space in Auroshilpam

1999 - National Vikas Jyoti Award, by WEDF - Excellence award for Individual Achievement for the growth of Indian economy.
- Gold medal, by ITPO, for excellence in presentation for construction in 66 hours of a disaster-resistant house.
- Bharat Excellence Award" and gold medal, and FFI - Excellence Award for "Outstanding leadership and extra-ordinary achievements in his field of work".
1998 - Bharthiya Nirman Ratan Award, by IEDRA - Excellence Award of Indian construction, for "Individual Outstanding Achievement and Nation Building".
1996 - Best Building Centre in India, by HUDCO, with the team of AV-BC for Outstanding Performance.
1995 - Best Building Centre in India, by HUDCO, with the team of AV-BC for Outstanding Performance.
1994 - Best Building Centre in India, by HUDCO, with the team of AV-BC for Outstanding Performance.
1992 - Hassan Fathy International Award for architecture for the poor given by Hassan Fathy Foundation. Also joint award with Suhasini Ayer for the Visitors Centre at Auroville.

Contact:
Earth Institute, Auroshilpam, Auroville 605101
Tel: 0413-2623064 or 2623330
e-mail: earthinstitute@auroville.org.in

Sigi Keller

Background:
Before coming to India, Sigi worked as a tool maker and then for many years in the planning and construction of mechanical devices in the electronics industry.
In 1975 he came to Auroville, where in 1987 he built his own house in Gaya. This was his first architectural experience.
In 1990 he started designing and constructing a series of small houses, which led to bigger and more complex buildings in terms of style and materials.

Q: How did you get into designing and building houses?
A: By coming to Auroville I was immediately fascinated by the Auroville architecture, because of the freedom it gave to bring totally new ideas and forms into life. I wanted to be involved and participate in this type of creation. However, in the first years here in Auroville I was busy in all kinds of other activities, such as tree planting, garden work, making jewellery, and working in metal workshops. I was also experimenting with, and building, alternative energy devices such as windmills, wind generators and other alternative forms of technology.
But then, after building our family house, I realised that that was what I wanted to do; and so four years later I started in that field of work.

Q: How do you approach architecture?
A: There are so many aspects to the design of a building. To bring all these to a unified whole is the goal.
In simple words: The task is to bring together all the forms, materials, spaces and levels in a harmonious way and style. Putting one's love, time and energy into a building makes the final result the more rewarding and gratifying; where one can say "Oh that feels good!"
It's simple but fascinating to bring down an idea or dream in my own or someone else's head, and make it manifest in material reality.

Contact: sigi@auroville.org.in

Residence   Sigi's house

Gundolf Zurmühl

When did you come to Auroville?
After earlier visits, I settled down here in 1987. Later I had some breaks for working in Germany, but I am back since 2000.

Background or some info on your training?
I studied architecture in Stuttgart, Germany. After visiting Auroville, I focused my further studies on architecture and town planning in tropical countries at Technical University, Berlin, with Diploma.

Some description of the nature of your work?
On a general level my work concentrates on contributing towards sustainability in architectural design / urban design / town planning.
On a practical level my concern is to unburden daily life from the constraints of our tropical environment, through clever and functional design concepts.

Through your work what are you trying to express?
Beauty and unity in diversity.

Evolution of work for Auroville:
● Architectural design work of residential buildings in Ravena, Samasti, Kottakarai and Discipline, 1987-91.
● Collaboration with Suhasini on Kindergarten project, 1992.

Doris's residence

● Collaboration with Satprem on 3rd phase of Vikas project, 1997.
● Collaboration with Axel: concept for seminar centre in Udayan, 1998.
● Participation in the team developing a concept for the Auroville Plaza, 2000.
● Since 2000, member of Aurofuture, now L'Avenir d'Auroville, working on general planning and CAD mapping.
● Architectural design work for a workshop in Samasti, and a workshop and residence in Angira's Garden, both in 2005.

● Collaboration with Helmut on 3rd & 4th phases of Savitri Bhavan, 2006.
● Participation in the "Dream Catcher" team, then on a concept for Crownways, 2007.

What architectural projects in Auroville do you appreciate most?
The Matrimandir and the work of Piero and Gloria

Contact: gundolf@auroville.org.in

Sonali Phadnis

Sonali came to Auroville in 1999 having graduated the same year from the University of Pune in India. She joined 'Kolam', an architecture unit headed by Anupama Kundoo, and worked there for 5 years. Later she became the executive architect of Kolam, and has been associated with Anupama in realising many projects in and around Auroville .

In the year 2008 she started her new studio 'Metamorphosis', and is still continuing the challenge of Auroville architectural practice which includes many projects, from house extensions to collective housing projects, office buildings etc.

In her own words...
I had the background of architectural education and almost no background of practical work experience.

I was fascinated to see the variety of experimentation and research done by early Auroville architects and non-architects under the challenging Master Plan, with a dream to build the city the earth needs.

When I started working in Kolam I enjoyed getting involved in the hands-on work, learning about the building materials and practices. The reward of the work was the process, and it gave me immense satisfaction watching the behaviour of building materials and the elements of the design taking shape.

Over the years as I've been growing as an Aurovilian and understanding Auroville at a deeper level, the approach towards architecture has been emerging. I dedicated my early years to explore the place as a whole and understand its different layers, the social and spiritual aspect.

This experience helps me now to face the challenges of working on the physical form better. I started doing small scale projects and took pleasure in working and learning from each of them.

Recently I've had the opportunity to design the most challenging residential projects in Auroville, which were also social experiments stimulating the idea of living in the city,
which is still missing in the existing architectural scenario.

I try to involve the climatic, ecological aspects in design and also like to explore with different building materials and technologies. My approach to architecture is the quality of space and balance of different elements of the design to create a balanced environment intended by the use of the project.

Citadines

Design experience in Auroville to date:
1. Extension of Samasti Guest House.
2. Extension of a residence in Petite Ferme.
3. Classrooms for Life Education Centre.
4. Isaiambalam Guest House.

5. Workshop and Office for Transport Service.
6. Sports Resource Centre,New Creation.
7. Auroville Foundation office building.
8. Citadyn, a collective housing project of 30 apartments, habitat area.

9. Inspiration, a collective housing project in habitat area. (Under construction)
10. Maitreye, a housing project in Residential Zone. (Under construction)
11. SAIIER office building.

Meeting hall of the Sri Aurobindo
World Centre for Human Unity (SAWCHU)
Life Education Centre

Inspiration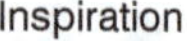

Shama Dalvi

Having graduated from the Goa College of Architecture in 1993, Shama Dalvi began her architecture profession as an apprentice in Auroville. Three years later, she started her own independent practice, 'Shama Dalvi Architects' (SDA), with a keen inclination to make environmental sensitivity a standing feature in her work.

Her designs are 'human-centric', focusing on the creation of practical and personalised spaces responsive to the user's needs and taking into account functionality, economic feasibility and site realities.

As an overall work ethic, her designs promote resource conservation by including energy efficiency and water conservation features, plus ways to reduce environmental impact through the use of local materials and alternative construction techniques. All alternative techniques used are derived from traditional methods of building, which have been improved upon with the help of enhanced modern technology and techniques. Strongly against extremism of any sort, a tasteful combination of techniques and built elements has become a well appreciated standard in her projects.

Contact: Shama Dalvi Architects, Aurelec, Auroville 605 101; Tel: 0413-2622128
www.shamadalvi.com
info@shamadalvi.com

Dharmesh Jadeja

My first trip to Auroville in 1992 was to explore its concept. The way Auroville has existed through its past, and enjoys unique status in India, was enough to take a decision to be part of this adventure.

My formal education was as a Civil Engineer from Birla Engineering College. Since my early years, indigenous building materials, techniques and locally appropriate aesthetics have been fields of interest. To bring these techniques into the mainstream rather than patronising them as "alternative" is my dream. Now I'm looking forward to networking with various Indian organisations in the country doing similar work, and trying to bring back the traditional knowledge of designing and building in India to suit contemporary needs. In 1996-97, I worked under Ray Meeker at Golden Bridge

Pottery in Pondicherry as an apprentice for Architectural Ceramics and fired house technique. This experience greatly enhanced the design sensibilities in my work.

Working in Auroville has been a process of unlearning and search rather than of any expression or achievement. Here one's ideas and work evolve with one as an individual, and the pace is rather accelerated. The challenges that you face here are fascinating, and your outer work reflects your inner search and conflicts. Challenges you face in your work are usually opportunities to overcome shortcomings.

I like exploring almost all forms of design, from architecture, interior design and landscape to product design, calligraphy, graphics and architectural ceramics & pottery. My search somehow has always

been to combine the various fields of design through the work I do, and explore how all these fields relate to each other and enhance the quality of the work. I like combining all these with strong aesthetics rooted in our culture, and using them in unusual ways. To me a good design incorporates, absorbs and relates to other forms of design and materials in it regardless of the field it belongs to. Architecture is one of the most fascinating fields of design.

Our work reflects the needs, aesthetics and life of the user rather than our expression of design expertise or techniques. Our design processes are very intensive, and the forms very basic, simple and non-intrusive to local aesthetics. They encompass the spaces that are conceptually rooted in Indian architecture yet feel contemporary.

Through my architecture, I try to go beyond it, almost become one with it and be part of that process in its totality. This way you merge the boundaries between the designer and the user, almost becoming non-existent when clients feel that it is their creation.

Aims and objectives of our office 'Buildaur':
● to achieve a synthesis between the traditional ways of designing and building the living environment, and contemporary life.
● to promote eco-friendly, climatically appropriate, energy efficient, cost effective building materials and techniques that utilise locally appropriate inputs and aesthetics.
● to work together with professionals from various fields of design while at the same time learning from each other's expertise to widen the base of knowledge.
● to propagate the use of sustainable building technologies and innovations by working with like-minded organisations, NGOs, institutions and individuals to form a network of knowledge centres throughout India.
● to use the arts, crafts and design in its work to create aesthetic and holistic living environments for the soul and spirit of their users.
● to dedicate ourselves to the ideal of unending education by various ways of learning & acquiring knowledge through research, interaction and enquiry.
● to be inspired by the ancient Indian wisdom and art of building, where the form is the creation of the spirit and draws all its meaning and value from the infinite spirit.

Works in and around Auroville:
● House for Self, Petite Ferme
● Atithi Griha guest house
● Kala Kendra, adaptive re-use, Bharat Nivas
● Indus Valley complex
● Arka (original concepts)
● Kottakarai Organic Food Processing Unit (original concepts)
● Swayam, residential project
● Various architectural and design projects outside Auroville.

Contact: DUSTUDIO, Bharat Nivas, Auroville 605 101, Tel: 0413-2623553, dharmesh@auroville.org.in

Pino Marchese

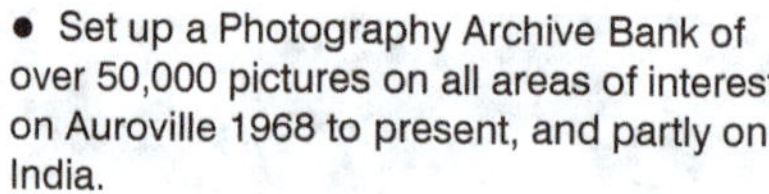

Background
Graduated in architecture from University of Florence in 1990.
Practised pottery at 'Antica Fornace Di Bacchereto' in Vinci-Tuscany, 1982-84.

Professional experience
- Worked in studios of architecture in south Italy and Florence doing projects for housing, commercial and public buildings, 1990-1998
- Independent practice in India, 1998, to present time, including innovative urban planning, sustainable architecture, landscape, interior and product design and photography.
- Part of the team in Auroville's Future – Town Planning & Centre for Urban Research, 1998-2005.
- Worked in close association with Auroville's chief architect Roger Anger on various planning and architecture projects, 1998 onwards.

Nature of work
- Innovative Urban Planning
- Sustainable Architecture
- Landscaping
- Interior & Product Design
- Photography
- Internships offered to students in architecture-related design fields

- Set up a Photography Archive Bank of over 50,000 pictures on all areas of interest on Auroville 1968 to present, and partly on India.

Contact: C&M Architects
Horizon, Auroshilpam, Auroville
Tel: 0413-262 2495, 2623 520
auropino@yahoo.it

Sheril Castelino

Graduated in architecture from Kamla Raheja Vidyanidhi Institute of Architecture & Environmental Studies in Bombay in 1997. Work experiments with study travels in India & Europe 1997-2000. Studied Italian cinema & literature in Perugia, Italy, in 2000.

Professional experience
- Independent practice in Architecture and Design Consultancy 2001to present day.
- Part of the Innovative Urban Planning team for Auroville's Future – Centre for Urban Research and assisted Auroville's chief architect Roger Anger 1997-2006.
- Active participant in various Planning & Development groups in Auroville.
- Assisted an art historian on research into the Lost Temples of Khajuraho.

Nature of work
- Independent architectural consultancy in keeping with socio-economic and environmental concerns. The projects are as far as possible eco-friendly in character, taking into account energy conservation factor and use of alternative forms of building technology wherever possible
- Interior & product design
- Landscape design
- Freelance architectural journalism - documenting regular developments in Auroville & Pondichery for Indian & international design journals
- Internships provided to Indian and international students in all design fields
- Organising and management of Seminars and Workshops for students and professionals in sustainable development practices
- Technology transfer of alternative building technology outside of Auroville

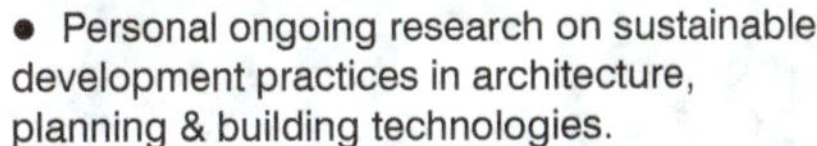

- Personal ongoing research on sustainable development practices in architecture, planning & building technologies.

Contact: e-mail: sheril@auroville.org.in

David Nightingale

I studied architecture at the University of Newcastle-upon-Tyne in England, and graduated in 1991 after a one year exchange with the TH Darmstadt in Germany.

I obtained work experience in Toronto, Canada, where I learned much about what I didn't want to do (i.e. shopping malls and office developments), and then in Berlin, Germany, where I learned more about what I did want to do (i.e. social housing and schools).

After travelling around the world looking for a more holistic environment in which to live and work, I settled in Auroville in 1997. Initially I worked in Auroville's Future for a couple of years until deciding to leave in 1999 to found 'Lines' with Ganesh Bala and Dominic Dube.

As 'Lines' morphed into 'Brand New Day' in 2001, I took a sabbatical from architecture for a couple of years, after which in 2003 I began working with Ganesh on the Integral Learning Centre in Vérité. Since its completion in 2005 we have been working on the designs for a number of new projects as well as helping to found the 'dreamcatchers' group.

Ganesh Bala

I studied Architecture in Bombay, graduating in 1997. During the course of my architectural studies I apprenticed with various offices in Bombay, with a special interest in the documentation and analysis of historic buildings in various parts of India. My involvement with Auroville began in 1997 in AuroFuture. This was followed by the founding of 'Lines' in 1999 with architects David Nightingale and Dominic Dube. For two years, beginning in 2001, I worked in 'Brand New Day'. A study exchange programme, which took me to Brazil in 2002, proved to be decisive in the refinement of my architectural explorations. In 2003, I began working with David on the Integral Learning Centre at Vérité. Apart from architectural practice, I have also been involved as the Editor of 'Realty', a magazine devoted to the construction industry. I also love painting and have held exhibitions in Auroville and Pondicherry.

Contact: ganesh_bala@hotmail.com

Vérité, Integral Learning Centre

Ray Meeker

(based in Pondicherry, but associated with Auroville)

On firing houses

"I spent 13 years firing houses. I have now stopped for several reasons, but in the main because I viewed the process as an experiment in the pursuit of an eco-friendly technology for low to moderate cost housing. In fact it proved to be too energy-intensive for sustainable development. But, living in the thrall of process - on technical as well as aesthetic levels - I continued to fire houses long after I realised that it was not going to work as I had hoped. There is nothing quite so exhilarating as a very large kiln; a series of six or eight volumes, connected with a winding tongue of flame - a roiling dragon of incandescent fire - restrained by an undulating roof-scape of mud vaults and domes.

As a potter - and pyromaniac of sorts - with a university background in architecture, living in a country with an acute housing shortage, I was drawn to the idea and then captivated by the process - and by the challenge - of making such a patently absurd notion work.

And it does work. I mean, it is possible to stabilise a mud house by firing it, and though the energy audit was not what I had hoped for, an aesthetic was born from the process that met with wide appeal. To fire what is essentially a large mud-walled kiln, full of heavy clay product bricks, tiles, drain pipes, etc, and finish it, post-firing, as a house, presents an unusual and extremely limiting set of design parameters. Mud. No tensile strength so no flat roofs. The dynamic load of thermal expansion while firing. Flame path continuity. And many others. But if a good brick clay is available on-site and a plentiful local fuel source is available, there are compelling reasons to make the attempt. Design complexity can be achieved by combining conventional technologies with a fired building core-casting r.c.c. lofts in high vaulted spaces or connecting several clusters of vaults and domes with conventional flat roofing techniques. And all manner of interesting terracotta can be fired along with the house and used in finishing.

My first test structure was a small vaulted room, three metres in length and two metres wide. Each year of testing brought new ideas. Firing efficiency was always the primary focus, and led to larger structures with common walls and connecting flues between rooms - not unlike standard multi-chambered kilns. But nobody really wants to live in a kiln. Going beyond the basics of firing efficiency to design a house always compromised fuel consumption. Very complex flame paths are out of the question, as all corners of the interior space must be well fired. Finally I began mixing coal dust into the brick of both product and structure. Six hours to ignite the coal layer in the base of the first chamber, then just let it burn at leisure. Five or six days later, open the doors, unload the fired product and start finishing.

Agni Jata fired house

This actually solved the problem of fuel consumption, but you sacrifice control of the fire. If you get it wrong you either underfire the structure or melt down the product brick, or both.

It has to be emphasised that without the general Auroville mindset - an openness to experiment - and specifically Mallika's and Satyajit's courage to take significant financial risks on what was a very new and relatively untested technology, it is unlikely that I would have been able to take fired building as far as I did. And while there were several larger projects done outside Auroville, it was in Auroville that virtually all my technical innovations developed.

Mallika's house, or 'Agni Jata', in Auroville, provided the first opportunity to take the process beyond the compound wall of the Golden Bridge Pottery in Pondicherry,

where my first six experimental structures had been fired. Agni Jata was the first fired house to be built for a client, and with four vaults surrounding a central dome it was my first attempt at firing a large, unconventional multi-chambered kiln. In Satyajit's house the attempt was to work with a more house-like floor plan. And I tried the canted wall - the

Process of firing a house

wall actually leans - to resist firing expansion, which proved effective both structurally and aesthetically.

So I owe a special thanks to Auroville, as a cradle of innovation."

Contact:
e-mail: raydeb2@gmail.com

Shailaja Sudhalkar Bhati

Background
Studied architecture in M. S. University, Baroda, Gujarat. Graduated in 1995 and worked for a couple of years in Chandigarh. Became a lecturer in a college of architecture for a year, before coming to Auroville in 1999. In Auroville, she works as an executive of PATH, along with Lalit Kishor Bhati, an architect and urban planner. PATH (Planning and Architecture Towards Holistic development) is a young architecture and planning studio in Auroville, endeavoring to create sustainable and harmonious designs in planning, architecture and interiors.

Nature of work?

Works by 'PATH' in and around Auroville and

Puducherry include
- Own house, 2004
- Nandanam Kindergarten, Centre Field, 2006 & 2010
- Renovation & interior of an office, Puducherry, 2005-06
- Residences near Auroville, 2007-2010
- Puducherry State Energy Park, 2007 - till date
- Stupa, near Auroville, 2010

Proposals
- Collective housing, Auroville, 2005
- Alternative design for Auroville Institute of Integral Health, Crown, Auroville, 2009

Through your work, what are you trying to find, or express? Please give some overview of the evolution of your work, and milestones on the way.

My work in design at Chandigarh opened up the facet of intuition in architecture, which generally does not come forth in conventional education. Inspired constantly by the mountain ranges in the background and the built environment carved out by Le Corbusier, it became clear that harmony has a very high influence on the minds of the observer, and that an architect's role goes much beyond 'building'.

In Auroville, where work in every field is a meditative exploration, I found myself in the midst of a rich legacy of experimentation and innovation. My work in Auroville started with a look inward, a search within my soul, for depending on the quality of inner space was the expression of outer forms.

I find this process to be very interesting, for the more one refines oneself, the more one is impersonal and transparent, to give living

form to the space that needs to come. For the design is there; the aspiration is there, too. And so is the need of the earth. An architect is only a means to the fulfillment…. After all, what exactly it is that one is trying to find or express is not a matter of importance. It is the attempt to rise above oneself, go beyond personal limitations and walk with faith into the unknown that the unfolding and creating is all about.

Which of your works best expresses your vision and philosophy?

Each work, however large or small, does. Still, very close to my heart is Nandanam Kindergarten, which forms the base of my work. Here, while listening very intently to the requirements, I became aware that I actually had 4 clients, besides the Mother: the earth at the site, the children, the client body of teachers and the building itself.

Each had to be listened to, for silently each told me what I needed to do. It was simultaneously a humbling and empowering experience to balance each one's needs and be a part of creating fun-filled harmonious spaces.

Another project I must mention is the Stupa. Since an architect's work leads her or him to work on earth and use and mould its gifts in different ways, it is extremely fortunate to be a part in the making of a structure that is meant to hold healing energies.

Contact:
Courage Community, Auroville 605 101.
Tel: 0413-2623633
Email:shailaja@auroville.org.in

Ananda

(based in Pondicherry, but associated with Auroville)

What major projects have you been responsible for?

For us, all projects are major. Auroform, which has been in existence since 1976, has done hundreds of projects all over India, and also a couple abroad. Mainly we work for leading industrialists, film celebrities, on high-end residences, and so on, but we also do a few offices, clubs and hotels.

Though the quality of the finish and design is much superior in our "outside" projects, we do have the great joy of being able to offer our honorary services to several Auroville works also. Since the last couple of years we have been face-lifting existing buildings in New Creation settlement and adding a few new ones. Also we designed the swimming pool facility there. Further, we are lucky enough to be able to contribute in a small way to the Matrimandir work, and recently have been entrusted with a residential complex in the city centre.

Though at present it is easier to manifest projects outside Auroville, it would be a dream indeed to be able to offer our work in the township...when the conditions are right.

Through your work what are you trying to find or express?

The very fact that we are here in the Ashram or Auroville means we have something special to give. Consciously or unconsciously we are the instruments of her grace, and the more transparent we become, the more this smile, this presence, this peace can make a home in all one does and touches.

Of course one could also say in terms of design that we try to reduce and reduce ever more till we reach the essence of things and spaces, and so create something vibrant and full in a minimalistic simplicity...but the very truth of the search is to become an instrument, impersonal and sincere, and "sharpened" enough to incarnate a drop of this ocean of beauty which is trying to manifest itself.

Which of your works best expresses your vision or philosophy?

Well, we did do a few houses, mainly in Hyderabad, where there is a living presence which moistens one's eyes from the gratitude rising from the heart...it is a beautiful feeling. I can't give the names of the clients...

Please give us an overview of the evolution of your work and the milestones on the way.

We started over 30 years ago by doing a few furniture pieces...in Auroville actually, and from there moved on to doing interiors, and later on to architectural projects.

We have since been working with several Aurovilians to add to and complement our work. The most notable has been our collaboration with Pierre Legrand, as his art has given a new dimension to the spaces we create. Together with him we were able to create spaces and dimensions within spaces. Though self-sufficient in its manifestion, the art once integrated in the whole is no more a separate "oddity" but more like notes in a symphony. It has been a very rewarding experience, as the result is often stunning, and we are just at the beginning of a long path of new experiences. Also what would a house be out of context? Landscape designing is the perfect utilisation of the surroundings and the link between the building and the environment. Working with Kalyamurthy from "Progress" in New Creation added this dimension to our work too. As stated, after all these years one still feels at the beginning of everything, as so much remains to be done.

Which architectural projects in Auroville do you appreciate most?

The Master Plan... Matrimandir... Auromodele.

Contact: Auroform, Ph: 0413-2334727, 2334698, auroform@auroville.org.in

Houses in New Creation settlement

Meera Prajapati

When did you come to Auroville?
My first visit to Auroville was in the year 2000, but I came again in 2004 searching for deeper and more meaningful connection in life and work. I joined Auroville in 2007/8.

Background and training
I graduated as an architect from TVB School of Habitat Studies, New Delhi, in 2003. For one year I worked as an assistant architect in New Delhi with two architects and afterwards, for another year worked as project architect with a Dutch firm based in Delhi. In 2004 I started my first independent project, which was in Auroville.

Nature of work in Auroville
My work in Auroville has followed two different lines of growth. One is in the field of designing independent buildings and the other is in the area of urban planning and design. My first work in Auroville was building of Bliss, a house inspired by traditional tropical architecture, in 2004/5, followed by building of the extension for Upasana Design Studio. In the meantime I also engaged myself for the complete architectural archiving of Matrimandir. Later I did some more residential buildings and then moved on to urban planning and design by joining L'avenir.

Through your work what are you trying to find or express?
Sustainability in its integrity has been the key interest in my architectural explorations. Harmony of built form and nature, material and technique in its true potential, functionality of forms, cost effectiveness, simplicity, and interpretation of cultural continuity of tropical architecture are some facets that have repeatedly found expression in my work.

Contact: meera@auroville.org.in

Resident house in Angira's Garden Upasana

Resident house in Samasti

Resident house in Bliss ▼

Anita

In 1994, as a final year student of architecture, I found myself here in Auroville, and that's when my real learning began....as a designer, architect....and most importantly as a person! Having worked with the AV Building Centre for 8 years on projects like the Solar Kitchen and Prarthna row housing, amongst others, my interests have evolved and diversified to city planning, residents' participation, mediation, massage, motherhood and cooking!

Contact: anita@auroville.org.in

Poonam Mulchandani

Born in Mumbai on May 10th 1975, Poonam Mulchandani moved to Auroville in 1997, shortly after graduating from the Kamla Raheja Institute for Architecture and Environmental Studies. She has had an independent practice since then, indulging in diverse projects, all of them incorporating sustainable design practices while maintaining cost and time efficiency. She most enjoys working on public / educational buildings and projects with a social purpose. Architecture for her is a celebration of form, lines, light, colour and nature.

Design directives:
To create a contemporary architectural language, using a vocabulary of the vernacular.

To diminish the distinction between the natural and the built.

To evolve an architectural expression through simplicity in form, lines and function.
Sustainable practice strategies:
Climate response:
● Raised floors to enhance air flow and avoid humidity.
● Large openings for ample air flow.
● Shading of outer walls.
● Roof insulation.
● Use of "passive cooling" design principles like "stack effect".

Material sensibility:
● Use of rammed earth foundations, load bearing structural systems to reduce the use of concrete, and thus CO_2 emissions. (One ton of CO_2 is released during the production of one tonne of cement)
● Mud plaster for external rendering to reduce thermal heat gain.
● Use of salvaged timber for roof structure, doors and windows.
● Use of prefabricated RCC elements for time, cost and water efficiency.

Water conservation:
● Use of dry composting toilets.
● Waste water recycling and reuse.
● Rainwater harvesting.
● Use of indigenous species of vegetation for landscaping.

Energy conservation:
● Use of solar energy to generate electricity and heat water.

Contact:
poonam@auroville.org.in
www.poonam-mulchandani.com

Annadana seed bank

Studio house in Repos

Environment education centre

SacredGroves

Why?

There is an acute shortage of affordable housing in Auroville, which deters many good people from joining the community. The SacredGroves project was conceived to alleviate this problem with the construction of 108 new homes for Newcomers, Aurovilians and long-term volunteers, in a manner consistent with the Mother's vision for Auroville.

How?

The project is designed to be a model of ecological community living using ecologically sensitive construction methods. We hope this model can be replicated in high density urban areas in India and elsewhere.

Ecological community living

Many of the problems of earth, soul and society are caused by the high-earning, high-pressure, high-carbon individualistic urban lifestyle that so many people lead. Instead, we offer the opportunity for a simpler, more self-sufficient yet inter-dependent and ecological way of living that allows more time for family, community and the nourishment of the soul.

We aim to achieve this by providing low-cost, low-maintenance, off-grid ecological housing incorporating the following elements:

- Energy self-sufficiency using solar, wind, pumped storage and bio-mass systems.

- Water self-sufficiency from rainwater and grey-water harvesting.

- Some food self-sufficiency from the provision of organic vegetable gardens for each house.

- Preservation of forest areas – the sacred groves.

- Thick walls and passive cooling system negate the need for A/C and even fans.

- Composting toilets.

- Shared spaces and utilities to encourage community activities and interdependence.

Ecological construction

The construction industry in India is responsible for huge ecological problems. Illegal mining and quarrying are destroying vast areas of forests and hills. The indiscriminate dumping of construction and demolition (C&D) waste into wetland areas surrounding our cities results in the drying up of essential water bodies and aquifers. The dredging of sand from rivers alters their flow and adversely affects aquatic life.

The SacredGroves project offers an alternative model of construction by way of the following:

Re-using waste building rubble (from various Auroville and Pondicherry sites, including the Matrimandir) to construct houses made of earth concrete – a much less cement-intensive building material.

Re-cycling wood from packing crates.

Re-using discarded petrol pump pipes for shuttering.

Re-using tetrapak cartons to make innovative furniture.

Being mindful of our own construction waste by re-using, re-cycling and composting as much as possible.

Being mindful of our own use of scarce resources like energy and water.

mango@auroville.org.in
http://thesacredgroves.wordpress.com/

"I want to build a bridge between the local building culture and contemporary, modern architecture."

Fabian Ostner, a young architect (born 1968) from Germany, started to walk this bridge when he came to Auroville in August 1994. But what has an ambitious architect to seek for in rural south India? This is how it all started...

Understanding the components of life

I feel free to experiment with any material available, be it earth, concrete, steel, glass, aluminium or plastic, as each of them has its own qualities and aesthetics. I believe that there are no negative or positive materials; it all depends on how you use them.

I love architecture, as it is all about understanding the components of life and the possibilities of communication between so many involved beings. I am very glad to work with a team where design discussions and joy are part of the day to day experience…"

Building experience in Auroville to date

● Construction and site supervision of parts of the former Mirramukhi school in 1994-95.
● The German Pavilion, a conceptual project, as thesis work in 1997.
● A house in Prarthna, a flexible steel structure as an attempt to create interesting and aesthetic living spaces using industrial materials.
● Semi-collective housing project in Auromodèle (not realised).
● A house in Auromodèle - a hybrid and structurally challenging construct made of massive and light materials.

Contact: Fabian Ostner Architecture
Email: fabian.ostner@gmail.com
www.fabian-ostner-architecture.com

Second aluminium-clad house, Prarthna

Architects who have contributed to Auroville

Anupama Kundoo

Anupama Kundoo graduated in 1989 from the University of Bombay and practiced as an independent architect from 1990 onwards, producing a number of award-winning projects in which sustainable building technologies and infrastructural systems were developed as an integral part of the architecture. Auroville's Town Hall Complex, SAWCHU, Creativity Urban Eco-Community and Sangamam Low-Cost Housing Complex are some examples of her built work.

She completed her doctoral studies in 2008 at the University of Technology in Berlin, where she has been teaching architecture and urban management. Prior to that she taught at the Architectural Association School of Architecture, London, and the University of Technology, Darmstadt, and has lectured and conducted workshops in several other institutions.

Anupama Kundoo has been involved with Auroville's Planning and Urban Design work in close association with Roger Anger, and was responsible for the 'Master Plan: Perspective 2025' that was jointly produced with the Town and Country Planning Organisation, Government of India, Ministry of Urban Development and Poverty Alleviation, and has been recently gazetted. She has also produced the detailed urban design for Auroville's Admininstration Zone and its habitat area and the City Centre of Auroville, along the lines of which the recent projects are being developed. She has recently authored the book, 'Roger Anger, Research on Beauty: Architecture 1953-2008' that was jointly published by Jovis Verlag Berlin and the Indian Council of Architecture.

Anupama currently teaches Environmental Technology and Material Sciences, at Parsons The New School for Design in New York.

Residence houses

Dominic Dube

Background, or some info on your training?
Study started in Canada, where I was born.
Second step in Rome. I came to Auroville in
1996.
Some description of the nature of your work?
Simplicity and purity.
*Through your work, what are you trying to
seek, or express?*
To express beauty in permanence through
matter.
*Which of your works best expresses your
vision, or philosophy?*
Inge's house in Kottakarai, Auroville.
*Please give some overview of the evolution of
your work; milestones on the way*
Evolutionary process through art,
architecture and humanity.
*Which architectural projects in Auroville do
you appreciate most?*
Piero & Gloria's first projects in Certitude.

First section of the
'Line of Force' apartments complex

◀ Houses in Courage settlement

Architect: Dominic Dube

Resident house, Angiras Garden

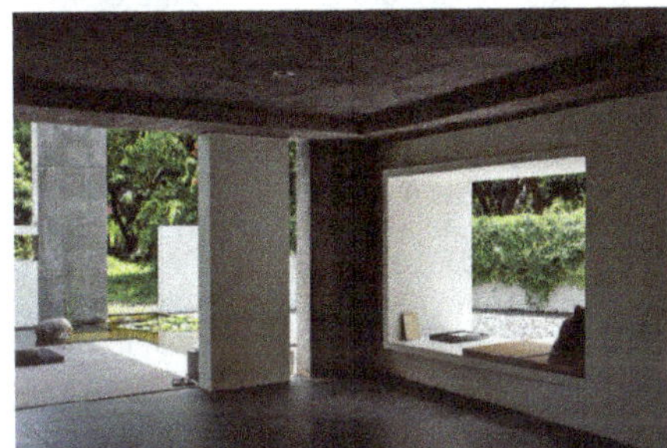

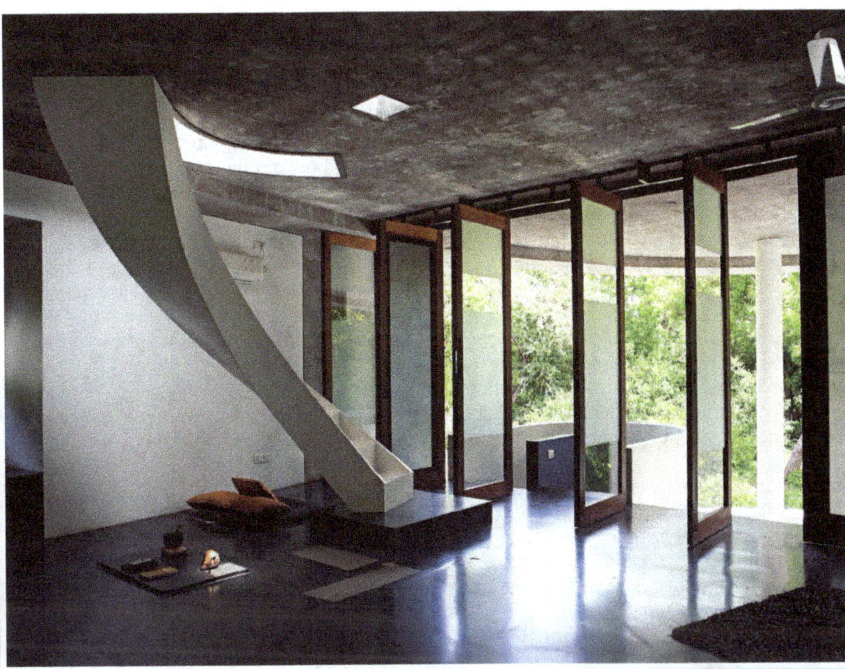

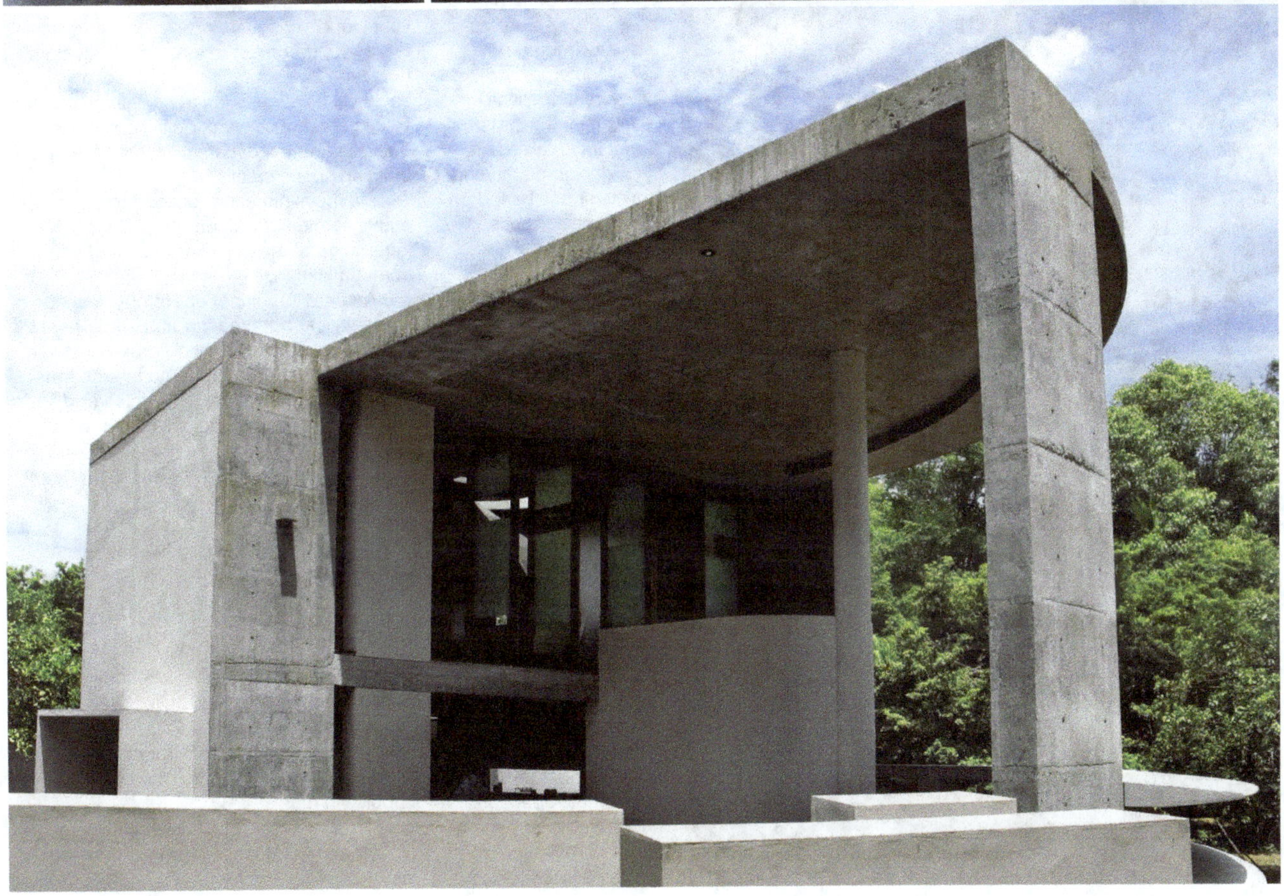

Jana Dreikhausen

Background or some Information on your training?
I studied Architecture, Philosophy, Art History and Urban Planning in Germany. After that I researched in passive solar energy in Israel, followed by teaching and practical experience in town planning and architectural design.

What are you trying to express through your work?
Architecture is a complex happening for me where the real task is to create space, where man is in contact with his inner potential and spiritual development.

Some description of your work in Auroville?
I have responded to multiple tasks, from landscape design to urban planning, organisational concepts and architectural and design, as well as academic research in multicultural communication patterns and the influence of architectural elements on human interaction.

Which works best express your vision or philosophy?

I enjoy most to work on town planning proposals for the development of Auroville, which are based on a concept of "flexibility in time and space"- open to inclusive participation and an open planning process.

The galaxy city model represents for me a complex organisation of energy and consciousness, challenging an integrating 'growing movement' from the individual to the collective, as a prelude to a new human interaction on all levels.

The movement of a city taking shape in this way can only define itself in a spirit that fosters a playful evolution of innovative ways of life, where all vivid forces are concentrated on the present, open to an ongoing future process.

My architectural work concentrates on partial planned space building elements, creating the best possible opportunities for an open display - encouraging to blossom with creative ease into new expressions, facilitating

unexplored or surprising possibilities as well as a perfect living quality at every moment or development phase - ready to spring into ever new future realisations.

I design public and private space based on this architectural philosophy of consciousness, transformation and sustainability, as space creation for innovative living and working, interacting, sharing and communicating with each other in an atmosphere of freedom and openness, where people find a natural, joyful connection to the centre within themselves, the multicultural community and the city centre, the raison d'être.

Architecture is a complex happening for me, where the concrete architectural projects create the appropriate space for an 'open development' and an ever evolving consciousness.

The design for the new Auroville Language Laboratory best expresses my research in the interaction of space and sound as patterns of energy, which are - like in the city galaxy - connected to universal forces, building an ideal atmosphere for our multilingual community to study, teach and communicate. It is a contemporary urban public building, combining the contemporary space quality and high tech, integrating alternative energy into a sustainability concept.

The residential buildings in Sukhavati give practical evidence of my focus to orientate architecture as well into the Galaxy Plan's underlying energy pattern, as into the physical landscape and body of the city. The buildings were designed using a prototype of a self-developed passive cooling system, as my response to sustainability and our climatic conditions. The system centres on the specific use of ventilation, and was simulated by computer, as though the building was a boat in the sea without wind.

Please give some overview of the evolution of your work?
Starting from an interest in architectural language and expression as reflection of society, I have questioned social and political values and conscience, definitions of life qualities and the dynamic initiated through building space creations.

My main interest is focused to explore man's spiritual development ability of inner understanding, interaction and communication.

Architecture is not about physical space alone, but about creating an atmosphere of consciousness, initiating growing awareness of perception and interaction, opening up the freedom of choice and responsibility, authenticity within and with creation. Contact with the inner potential fosters joy, simplicity and perfection, beauty and sustainability.

I am compassionate to study the impact of architectural space on how man relates within, how it initiates the dynamic with each other and the creative process of inner and outer development.

This ongoing research offers ever new explorations in human relations, consciousness and my architectural expression.

Space only has quality for me if it creates an atmosphere which nourishes the creative impulse in man.

Contact: jana@auroville.org.in

Contact details

General information on Auroville:
info@auroville.org.in

Guest information & accommodation:
avguests@auroville.org.in
www.aurovilleguesthouses.org

Joining Auroville:
entry@auroville.org.in

Media relations:
outreachmedia@auroville.org.in

Auroville International website:
www.auroville-international.org

Auroville Foundation:
(Statutory body under Govt. of India)
Administrative Centre, Auroville - 605 101,
Tamil Nadu - INDIA
Tel: +91-413-2622-222, 2622 414
Fax: +91-413-2623-496
foundation@aurovillefoundation.org

**Working Committee of the
Residents Assembly of Auroville:**
Town Hall, Administrative Area,
Auroville - 605 101, Tamil Nadu - INDIA
Tel: +91-413-2622250
Fax: +91-413-2622055
wcoffice@auroville.org.in

Auroville website:
www.auroville.org

Acknowledgements

Photographs:
John Mandeen.
Other photos have been contributed by
individual architects; Auroville Archives
(Auroville's early years); Dominique Darr;
Giorgio (the Matrimandir interior and Inner
Chamber).

Text:
Text on pages 24-31 from the book
Roger Anger, Research on Beauty,
Recherche sur la beauté, Architecture 1953-
2008, Anupama Kundoo
with kind permission from Anupama Kundoo
and Jovis Verlag GmbH, Kurfürstenstraße
15/16, 10785 Berlin, Germany
www.jovis.de

Text on pages..... Meet the Architect ,
Interview with Roger Anger, the architect of
Auroville, from equals one, city, 1968

Designed and produced by:
PRISMA, Aurelec-Prayogashala,
Auroville 605101, Tamil Nadu, INDIA
prisma@auroville.org.in
Tel: +91-413-2622296
Fax: +91-413-2622185

D.T.P. work: S. Janarthanan

© PRISMA
Fifth edition: 2014

Disclaimer

While every effort has been made to ensure
accuracy in the text prior to publication,
PRISMA wishes to make it clear that Auroville
is a place of constant change, and it is
possible that certain details may no longer
be fully accurate at the time of purchase
of this publication. It should also be noted
that viewpoints expressed here are not
necessarily shared by the executives of
PRISMA or the inhabitants of the Auroville
township in general.

Front Cover:

Savitri Bhavan and Maitreye II

Back Cover:

Realization and Luminosity Apartments

Flap inside back Cover:

Inspiration Apartments and Savitri Bhavan
Hostel

Photos on right:

Clockwise from top left: Afsanah Guest
House, architect: Poppo Pingel; Auromodèle,
architect: Roger Anger; Exhibition Hall at
Visitors Center; residence in residence,
architect: Mona Pingel; Udavi School,
architect: Poppo Pingel; New Era Secondary
School; 'Town Hall' interior, architects: Roger
Anger & Anupama

International Publications

Auroville Architecture
by Franz Fassbender

Auroville Form Style and Design
by Franz Fassbender

Landscapes and Gardens of Auroville
by Franz Fassbender

Inauguration of Auroville
by Franz Fassbender

Auroville in a Nutshell
by Tim Wrey

Death doesn't exist
The Mother on Death, Sri Aurobindo on Rebirth
Compiled by Franz Fassbender

Divine Love
Compiled by Franz Fassbender

Five Dream
by Sri Aurobindo

Vision
Compiled by Franz Fassbender

Passage to More than India
by Dick Batstone

The Mother on Japan
Compiled by Franz Fassbender

Children of Change: A Spiritual Pilgrimage
by Amrit (Howard Shoji Iriyama)

Memories of Auroville - told by early Aurovilians
by Janet Feran

The Journeying Years
by Dianna Bowler

Auroville Reflected
by Bindu Mohanty

Finding the Psychic Being
by Loretta Shartsis

The Teachings of Flowers
The Life and Work of the Mother of the Sri Aurobindo Ashram
by Loretta Shartsis

The Supramental Transformation
by Loretta Shartsis

The Mother's Yoga - 1956-1973 (English & Frech)
Vol. 1, 1956-1967 & Vol. 2, 1968-1973
by Loretta Shartsis

Antithesis of Yoga
by Jocelyn Janaka

Bougainvilleas PROTECTION
by Narad (Richard Eggenberger), Nilisha Mehta

Crossroad The New Humanity
by Paulette Hadnagy

Die Praxis Des Integralen Yoga
By M. P. Pandit

The Way of the Sunlit Path
William Sullivan

Wildlife great and small of India's Coromandel
by Tim Wrey

A New Education With A Soul
Marguerite Smithwhite

Featured Titles

Divine Love

The texts presented in this book are selected from the Mother and Sri Aurobindo.

"Awakened to the meaning of my heart. That to feel love and oneness is to live. And this the magic of our golden change, is all the truth I know or seek, O sage."

Sri Aurobindo, Savitri, Book XII, Epilog

A Vision by the Mother

On 28th May 1958, the Mother recounted a vision she once had of a wonderful Being of Love and Consciousness, emanated from the Supreme Origin and projected directly into the Inconscient so that the creation would gradually awaken to the Supramental Consciousness. The Mother's account of this vision was brought out a first time in November 1906, in the Revue Cosmique, a monthly review published in Paris.

A Dream – Aims and Ideals of Auroville
the Mother on Auroville

50 years of Auroville from 28.02.1968 - 28.02.2018
Today, information about Auroville is abundant. Many people try to make meaning out of Auroville – about its conception, to what direction should we grow towards, and, what are we doing here?

But what was Mother's original Dream and what was her Vision for Auroville back then?

Matrimandir Talks by the Mother

This book presents most of Mother's Matrimandir talks, including how she conceived the idea for this special concentration and meditation building in Auroville.

Memories of Auroville - Told by early Aurovilians

Memories of Auroville is a book about the very early days of Auroville based on interviews made in 1997 with Aurovilians who lived here between 1968 and 1973. The interviews presented in this book are part of a history program for newcomers that I had created with my friend, Philip Melville in 1997. The plan was to divide Auroville's history into different eras and then interview Aurovilians according to their area of knowledge. Our first section would cover the years from 1968 till 1973 when the Mother was still in her physical body.

The Way of the Sunlit Path

May The Way of the Sunlit Path be a convenient guide for activating this ancient truth as a support for a Conscious Evolution.
May it illumine the transformation offered to us in the Integral Yoga.

A Dream Takes Shape (in English, French, Hindi)

A comprehensive brochure on the international township of Auroville in, ranging from its Charter and "Why Auroville?" to the plan of the township, the central Matrimandir, the national pavilions and residences, to working groups, the economy, making visits, how to join, its relationship to the Sri Aurobindo Ashram, and its key role in the future of the world. This brochure endeavours to highlight how The Mother envisioned Auroville from its inception, some of the major achievements realised over the years, and some of the difficulties currently faced in implementing the guidelines which she gave.

Mother on Japan

I had everything to learn in Japan. For four years, from an artistic point of view, I lived from wonder to wonder. And everything in this city, in this country, from beginning to end, gives you the impression of impermanence, of the unexpected, the exceptional... ...everything in this city, in this country, from beginning to end, gives you the impression of impermanence, of the unexpected, the exceptional. You always come to things you did not expect; you want to find them again and they are lost – they have made something else which is equally charming.

Auroville Reflected

On 28 February 1968, on an impoverished plateau on the Coromandel Coast of South India, about 4,000 people from around the world gathered for a most unusual inauguration. Handfuls of soil from the countries of the world were mixed together as a symbol of human unity. Why did Indira Gandhi, the erstwhile Prime Minister of India, support this development for "a city the earth needs?" Why did UNESCO endorse this project? Why does the Dalai Lama continue to be involved in the project? What led anthropologist Margaret Mead to insist that records must be kept of its progress? Why did both historian William Irwin Thompson and United Nations representative Robert Muller note that this social experiment may be a breakthrough for humanity even as critics commented, "it is an impossible dream"?

A House For the Third Millennium

Essays on Matrimandir

Nightwatch at the Matrimandir...

A cosmic spectacle; the black expanse above, the big black crater of Matrimandir's excavation carved deep into the soil. The four pillars - two of which are completed and the other two nearing completion - are four huge ships coming together from the four corners of the earth to meet at this pro propitious spot...

Passage to More than India

This book is a voyage of discovery. In 1959 the author, Dick Batstone, a classically educated bookseller in England, with a Christian background, comes across a life of the great Indian polymath Sri Aurobindo, though a series of apparently fortuitous circumstances. A meeting in Durham, England, leads him to a determination to get to the Sri Aurobindo Ashram in Pondicherry, a former French territory south of Madras.

www.ingramcontent.com/pod-product-compliance
Lightning Source LLC
Chambersburg PA
CBHW060232120726
48009CB00004B/239